100 THINGS TO DO IN WEST VIRGINIA BEFORE YOU DIE

Glade Creek Grist Mill

100
THINGS TO DO IN
WEST VIRGINIA
BEFORE YOU
DIE

MELODY PITTMAN AND ANGELA RICHARDS

Copyright © 2023 by Reedy Press, LLC
Reedy Press
PO Box 5131
St. Louis, MO 63139, USA
www.reedypress.com

No part of this publication may be reproduced or transmitted in any form or by any means, electronic or mechanical, including photocopy, recording, or any information storage and retrieval system, without permission in writing from the publisher.

Permissions may be sought directly from Reedy Press at the above mailing address or via our website at www.reedypress.com.

Library of Congress Control Number: 2022949259

ISBN: 9781681064291

Design by Jill Halpin

Photos by author unless otherwise noted.

Printed in the United States of America
23 24 25 26 27   5 4 3 2 1

We (the publisher and the author) have done our best to provide the most accurate information available when this book was completed. However, we make no warranty, guarantee, or promise about the accuracy, completeness, or currency of the information provided, and we expressly disclaim all warranties, express or implied. Please note that attractions, company names, addresses, websites, and phone numbers are subject to change or closure, and this is outside of our control. We are not responsible for any loss, damage, injury, or inconvenience that may occur due to the use of this book. When exploring new destinations, please do your homework before you go. You are responsible for your own safety and health when using this book.

DEDICATION

John Denver's "Take Me Home, Country Roads" is heard, sung, and known worldwide; it has inspired millions of people to wonder about the majestic place we call home. Our book is dedicated to those who have felt the pride in their hearts singing about "Almost Heaven, West Virginia," and those who wish to and will experience it in the future.

Ellen's Ice Cream

CONTENTS

Acknowledgments................................. xii

Preface... xiv

Food and Drink

1. Change Your Life with a Tudor's Biscuit 2
2. Indulge in Delicious Steak and Seafood at Chop House 3
3. Eat West Virginia Hot Dogs 4
4. Sip Local Wine at Batton Hollow 6
5. Taste the Best Brunch Chicken and Waffles 7
6. Nosh on Incredible Italian Food 8
7. Get the Scoop on the Best WV Ice Cream Shop 10
8. Chow Down at Secret Sandwich Society 11
9. Feed Your Appetite with Amazing Barbecue at Dem 2 Brothers ... 12
10. Sample Smooth Ambler Spirits 14
11. Dine at a Nostalgic Carhop Eatery 16
12. Feast at Thyme Bistro 18
13. Fill Up at the Wonder Bar Steakhouse 19
14. Satisfy Your Sweet Tooth at Local Pastry Shops 20
15. Channel Your Inner Foodie at Taste of Our Town 22
16. Drink a Cold One at Pies & Pints 23
17. Gather with Friends for Fine Dining at the Press Room 26
18. Stay in a European-Reminiscent Inn 27

Music and Entertainment

19. Secure Your Ticket to the West Virginia State Fair............. 30
20. Listen to Great Live Music in Thomas 31
21. Relax after Work at Haddad Riverfront Park.................. 32
22. Encounter the Unimaginable at TALA 33
23. Try Your Hand at Bingo.................................... 34
24. Sit under the Stars for a Performance 36
25. Play or Rock Out at the Clay Center 38
26. Reminisce at Camden Park 40
27. Uncover WV's Quirkiest Attraction: The Mystery Hole......... 41
28. Prowl around at Hovatter's Wildlife Zoo..................... 42
29. Attend a Mountain Stage Concert 43
30. Journey through Organ Cave 44
31. Treat Yourself to a Salt Spa Experience 45
32. Place Your Wager in Charles Town......................... 46

Sports and Recreation

33. Tee Up at the Best WV Golf Courses 50
34. Witness WV's Only National Park 52
35. Picnic at Coopers Rock State Forest 53
36. Sit Courtside at a WVU Basketball Game.................... 54
37. Cozy into a Cabin at the Ashland Resort..................... 55
38. Plunge West Virginia's Impressive Whitewater Rapids 56
39. Take a Scenic Train Ride in Elkins 57
40. Give Rock Climbing a Chance at Seneca Rocks................ 58

41. Go Stargazing in Hillsboro. 60
42. Chant "We Are Marshall" at a Home Game 62
43. Smell the Roses at Ritter Park 64
44. Sleep Outdoors at Watoga 65
45. Hit the Slopes at Snowshoe 66
46. Celebrate the Holiday Spirit at Oglebay Resort 68
47. Float on Down the River in St. Albans 69
48. Ride the Hatfield-McCoy Trail System 70
49. Splash around Summersville Lake. 72
50. Pedal a Recycled Railway Line 73
51. Have a Fantastic Stay at Stonewall Resort. 74
52. Find Your Inner Thrill Seeker at ACE Adventure Resort 75
53. Fish at Bluestone Lake. 76
54. Tailgate a WVU Mountaineer Football Game. 77
55. Bathe in the Mineral Waters of Berkeley Springs. 78

Culture and History

56. Sign Up for a Free Blenko Glass Factory Tour 100
57. Admire the West Virginia State Capitol 102
58. Overnight at Hotel Morgan 104
59. Explore the Beckley Exhibition Coal Mine. 105
60. Awe over the Palace of Gold 106
61. Examine the Local Wildlife in Upshur County 108
62. Visit Bramwell's Millionaire Mansions. 110
63. Tour the Awesome West Virginia State Museum 112

64. Experience Appalachian Culture via Living History
at Heritage Farm. 113
65. Jaunt through the Museum of American Glass 114
66. Grab a Selfie with Don Knotts 115
67. Walk around Harpers Ferry: WV's Civil War Past 116
68. Push Your Frights to the Limits in Moundsville 117
69. Step Back in Time at Blennerhassett Island 118
70. Become Competent in Native Wildlife, Flora, and Fauna 120
71. Wander the Huntington Museum of Art 121
72. Pay Tribute to the Fallen Miners 122
73. Stop by the First African American World War I Memorial 123

Shopping and Fashion

74. Learn about World-Famous Fiesta Dinnerware. 126
75. Observe the World-Class Tamarack 128
76. Buy Local at Orr's Farm Market 130
77. Snag Some Goodies at the Bridge Road Shops 131
78. Participate in a Quilt Hop 132
79. Purchase Gourmet Food and Kitchenwares in Lewisburg 133
80. Check Out the Antique Shopping in Berkeley Springs 134
81. Shop Locally at Gritt's Farm 136
82. Fangirl at Barnwood Living 137
83. Hang Out at the Beloved Taylor Books 138
84. Immerse Yourself in Helvetia's International Flavor 139
85. Stroll through Historic Downtown Shepherdstown 140

Uniquely West Virginia

86. Expand Your Palate with a WV Tradition: Ramps 144
87. Navigate to the Highest Point in West Virginia. 145
88. Vacation at the Greenbrier Resort 146
89. Meet the Dolly Sods Wilderness Area. 148
90. Try the World-Famous Mountain State Finishing Salt 150
91. Road-Trip Kanawha Falls and Scenic Route 60 151
92. Practice Your Photography at Babcock State Park 152
93. Pay Homage to the First Mother's Day Site 153
94. Snack on the Iconic Pepperoni Roll. 154
95. Gain an Understanding of the Mothman Folklore. 156
96. Glimpse One of the World's Largest Things in Green Bank 157
97. Hike to the Fabulous Blackwater Falls Waterfall 158
98. Photograph the Smallest Church in the Lower 48. 160
99. Drive through a Covered Bridge 161
100. Investigate the WV Bigfoot Museum 162

Suggested Itineraries 165
Activities by Season 169
Index 172

ACKNOWLEDGMENTS

I've known since the sixth grade that someday I would publish a book. Little did I know that the career I began eight years ago as a travel writer and influencer would evolve into my first book showcasing the gorgeous state I am from. Though I moved from West Virginia a decade ago, I still find myself there a few times a year because the mountains truly call me home. Thanks to my husband, Eddie, for being understanding when I travel so much; my daughter, Peyton, for her extensive vocabulary and joining me on my travels; my son-in-law, Blake, for his support and sharing his wife, Taylor, my daughter/blog partner/biggest cheerleader, with me so often; and to Scarlett, my granddaughter, for being the one I want to make future memories with. Thanks to my devout *Wherever I May Roam* followers and the new ones we will pick up from this book for making my dream come true. I hope to meet you sometime during a book signing or event and chat about your best West Virginia finds.

—Melody

Thank you to my friends and family for your support and encouragement while writing this book; it has meant more than you know. I dedicate this book to my parents, brother, grandparents, aunts, uncles, and cousins (who are my bonus siblings), with whom I share a lifetime of happy memories camping, hiking, biking, playing in creeks, swimming in Sherwood Lake, and annual trips to the cabins at Watoga State Park, which was the foundation for my love of travel and exploring our Mountain State. To my sweet nephews, Matthew, Andrew, and Michael, I am so glad you love taking adventures with me, and I hope we have many more road trips.

—Angie

PREFACE

When I think of my beloved wild, wonderful West Virginia, I am reminded of the timeless traditions, her kind people, and stunning beauty; my heart nearly bursts with pride from calling this my home for 44 years.

With the current Appalachia movement, where things we West Virginians have known and loved for years are gaining popularity (ATV trails, whitewater rafting, Mothman, stargazing, farm-to-table dining, and bluegrass music), it makes me so happy for West Virginia's perfect position in tourism. When you drive our roads and highways, pay attention to the wondrous beauty around you, and don't just pass through—a few minutes to look around never hurt anyone. You just might find a reason to stick around even longer.

—Melody

The chance to highlight local businesses that are so important to the small towns around our state drew me to this project. My hope when you read this book is you will be inspired to plan a trip to our beautiful state, whether you've never been here or are from here and are learning for the first time about some of the great places our state has to offer.

Over the last 25-plus years, my job has allowed me to explore every back road in the state many times over; I'm always amazed that I can still find new places to visit. From the valleys to the mountaintops, West Virginia offers so many unique places to eat, shop, and explore, and I hope you enjoy them all.

—Angie

Writing this book has been a true labor of love, and having the opportunity to do so together, as dear friends, has meant the world to us.

—Melody and Angie

Chicken and Waffles at Black Sheep

FOOD AND DRINK

CHANGE YOUR LIFE
WITH A TUDOR'S BISCUIT

Tudor's is a West Virginia institution founded in 1980, offering Southern-style biscuits, all your favorite breakfast dishes, and homestyle dinner items. The locals call it Tudor's, though the full name is Tudor's Biscuit World. You will know if someone is from WV by that simple distinction alone.

The star item at Tudor's is the biscuit itself—soft and fluffy with a noticeable butter flavor. The most popular items include the Ron (sausage, egg, and cheese); the Mary B (bacon, egg, and cheese); beans and corn bread; the gravy platter; and the Peppi (pepperoni and melted cheese). Vegetarians should go for the fried apple biscuit—oh my! There are locations in West Virginia, Ohio, Florida, and Kentucky.

1506 Washington St. E, Charleston 25311
(304) 343-4026, tudorsbiscuitworld.com

INDULGE IN DELICIOUS STEAK AND SEAFOOD
AT CHOP HOUSE

The richly decorated and elegant Chop House in Charleston is one of the best date nights, celebration spots, and fine-dining restaurants in West Virginia. For your dining experience, expect perfectly cooked midwestern grain-fed USDA prime beef, spectacular seafood, the best beef Wellington ever, and a wide array of mouthwatering sides. Do yourself a favor and try the cheesy au gratin potatoes. Thank me later. For a special treat, try the seafood platter with oysters, shrimp, fresh lobster, and the best crab Louie you'll ever have. Or, go for a sweet option with the mouthwatering maple pecan bread pudding.

Every detail at Chop House, from the premium wine selection and illuminated menus to the monogrammed china, gas lamps, and beautiful artwork, is top-notch. Gluten-free menus are available. Garage, street, and valet parking are available.

1003 Charleston Town Center, Charleston 25389
(304) 344-3954, thechophouserestaurant.com

> **DID YOU KNOW?**
> Chop House has been a mainstay in Charleston for 22-plus years.

EAT WEST VIRGINIA HOT DOGS

Eating a West Virginia hot dog is like a rite of passage. We eat them with chili (no beans and sometimes referred to as hot dog sauce), slaw, mustard, and onions. It is worth noting that the slaw in WV is often yellow and flavored with mustard. You will find WV hot dogs all around the state, but one place sticks out to me as the best. Hot dogs from Chum's, a roadside eatery in Marmet just 15 minutes south of Charleston, offers window service and quick delivery on your mouthwatering hot dogs. The bun, wiener, and toppings work together for a fantastic comfort food item that is highly addictive.

Chum's is closed Saturdays and Sundays.

8315 MacCorkle Ave., Charleston 25315
(304) 949-2486

TIP
Yes, you can try the yellow slaw here.

MORE LOCAL EATERIES FOR WV HOT DOGS

Yann's Hot Dog Stand
300 Washington St., Fairmont 26554
(304) 366-8660, yanns-hot-dog-stand.edan.io

The Custard Stand
3945 Sutton Ln., Sutton 26601
(304) 765-6500
custardstand.com/flatwoods-west-virginia

Stewarts Original Hot Dogs
2445 Fifth Ave., Huntington 25703
(304) 529-3647, stewartshotdogs.com

Hillbilly Hot Dogs
6951 Ohio River Rd., Lesage 25537
(304) 762-2458, hillbillyhotdogs.com

Der Dog Haus
2000 Seventh St., Parkersburg 26101
(304) 422-7703, facebook.com/derdoghaus

Dave's Famous T&L Hot Dogs
605 Pike St., Shinnston 26431
(304) 371-3515, tandlhotdogs.com

SIP LOCAL WINE
AT BATTON HOLLOW

Owners Jim and Toni Kelley turned a longtime hobby into a successful career after Jim retired from the US Air Force. Batton Hollow Winery offers a wide range of wines, from sweet white to warm and cozy reds. Step into the tasting room, where Jim and Toni are so welcoming and inviting that you'll hate to leave. Jim is certified in winemaking from the University of California, Davis Extension. He has also taken sommelier classes and is very knowledgeable about wines and wine pairings. Jim's USAF career sent the couple to Italy for six years, and their Italian experience shines through in the wines and ambince of the tasting room.

    A large patio overlooks a wide-open field, which is a perfect setting for Friday Wine Down nights (see website for schedule), with live music, a food truck, and assorted local beers.

406 Woodstock Dr., Lost Creek 26385
(304) 745-5700, battonhollowwinery.com

TASTE THE BEST BRUNCH
CHICKEN AND WAFFLES

Sunday brunch is always a treat at Black Sheep Burrito and Brews in downtown Charleston and Huntington. Black Sheep has tasty food, Bad Shepherd Brewery craft beer (Charleston location), and clever menu items, but the brunch menu has an item that will really win you over. Chicken and waffles is a trendy dish found all over the country, inspired by the South.

Black Sheep does it well with attention to every detail, like sage-infused maple syrup, candied pecans, and candied jalapeños. The O.G., the official name of BSB's chicken and waffles, also uses their delicious honey-nut breaded fried chicken and tops the beautiful plate with fried onion straws. Bam, what a find! Or, try the Blanche Devereaux, with a waffle and chicken plus spiced peaches in syrup and honey butter.

Brunch is served Sundays from 11 a.m. to 3 p.m.

702 Quarrier St., Charleston 25301
(304) 343-2739, blacksheepwv.com/brunch

279 Ninth St., Huntington 25701
(304) 523-1555

NOSH
ON INCREDIBLE ITALIAN FOOD

Italian food is a delicious offering in the Mountain State. You will find some great places to eat a classic spaghetti dish with or without meatballs or more exotic pasta creations throughout the state, but Jim's Steak and Spaghetti House in Huntington stands out among them all.

Jim's has several portion sizes, giving you budget to go-for-broke options. Even the lunch portions come with bread and a salad or cup of soup. Jim's spaghetti sauce is made special by a certain smokiness, but there are plenty of close contenders. Jim's Steak and Spaghetti House has been in business since 1938.

920 Fifth Ave., Huntington 25701
(304) 696-9788, jimsspaghetti.com

DID YOU KNOW?

Jim's Steak and Spaghetti is the only restaurant in the state to win a James Beard Award. Jim's was named the 2019 America's Classics winner (Southeast region) by the James Beard Foundation.

OTHER PLACES TO EXPERIENCE EXCELLENT ITALIAN FOOD IN WV

Pasquale's
224 Harper Park Dr., Beckley 25801 (55 years)
(304) 255-5253, beckleyitalian.com

Undo's Family Restaurant
753 Main St., Benwood 26031 (69 years)
(304) 233-0560, undos.com/undos-benwood.html

Oliverio's Ristorante
507 E Main St., Bridgeport 26330 (32 years)
(304) 842-7388, oliveriosristorante.com

Rocco's Ristorante
252 Main St., Ceredo 25507 (40 years)
(304) 453-3000, roccosristorante.com

Leonoro's Spaghetti House
1507 Washington St. E, Charleston 25311
(107 years)
(304) 343-1851, leonorosspaghettihouse.com

Muriale's Italian Kitchen
1742 Fairmont Ave., Fairmont 26554 (53 years)
(304) 363-3190, muriales.com

Chirico's Ristorante
24 Main Ave., Logan 25601 (41 years)
(304) 752-8900, chiricosristorante.com

Colombo's Restaurant
1236 Seventh St., Parkersburg 26101 (68 years)
(304) 428-5472, mycolombos.com

GET THE SCOOP
ON THE BEST WV ICE CREAM SHOP

Ellen's Homemade Ice Cream is a downtown Charleston staple. Locals and visitors have been enjoying the delicious hand-scooped 14 flavors of goodness for over 25 years. Many area restaurants even serve Ellen's quality creamery products on their menus. The delectable menu choices range from ice cream, sherbet, and gelato to low-fat frozen yogurt and sorbet. The ice cream specialty treats, like hot fudge sundaes, malts, and banana splits, get my vote. Coconut lovers need to try Ellen's coconut ice cream; it can turn even someone who doesn't like coconut into a fan. Go figure—it is that good! Or be adventurous and try an egg cream with milk, carbonated water, and flavored syrup.

You can also grab a coffee, soup, sandwich, or salad at Ellen's and enjoy indoor or sidewalk seating. The Capitol Street location in downtown Charleston is primo. Ellen's is open year-round and daily.

225 Capitol St., Charleston 25301
(304) 343-6488, ellensicecream.com

CHOW DOWN
AT SECRET SANDWICH SOCIETY

If you ask West Virginians where their favorite sandwich shop is, Secret Sandwich Society in Fayetteville will most likely be their answer. Secret Sandwich Society is a fun and funky little spot with creatively named sandwiches that have locally sourced ingredients and tasty combinations. The pimento cheese fries are delicious, and my favorite sandwich, the Truman, is piled high with turkey, peach jam, and blue cheese spread. There are also gluten-free, vegetarian, and dairy-free menu choices. Besides notorious sandwiches, the burgers and salads are also on point.

Unfortunately, SSS had a fire in November 2020, but is reopening in February 2023. SSS's merch is artsy and clever; you may need to add a piece to your wardrobe.

103 Keller Ave., Fayetteville 25840
(304) 574-4777, secretsandwichsociety.com

FEED YOUR APPETITE
WITH AMAZING BARBECUE AT DEM 2 BROTHERS

After much hard work and great food, what started as a roadside meat-smoking business became one of Charleston's most popular and highest-rated restaurants. Dem 2 Brothers and a Grill on Charleston's West Side, Five Corners area, is an unassuming barbecue joint with incredible food, reasonable prices, and a vivid mural painted on the side of the building.

    Dem 2 Brothers and a Grill has been in the Kanawha Valley for 10 years, founded and owned by Adrian "Bay" Wright who started out street vending. His barbecue is ranked some of the best in the state, and whatever you order, you can't go wrong. The pork is tender, and the barbecue sauce—not too sweet and not too heavy. The macaroni and cheese and green beans are delicious, and so is the cabbage. The cabbage was my favorite. Save room for the yummy banana pudding.

423 Virginia St. W, Charleston 25302
(304) 400-4977, dem2brosgrill.com

DID YOU KNOW?
Dem 2 Brothers have been featured on Food Network.

SAMPLE
SMOOTH AMBLER SPIRITS

Smooth Ambler in Greenbrier County has bucked tradition and created an award-winning distillery quickly becoming well known in the whiskey industry. Smooth Ambler has a unique take on using sourced whiskey from other states and blending them to make a truly one-of-a-kind bold flavor for their Old Scout Bourbon and Rye Whiskey. The Founders Cask Strength Series is made from ingredients sourced from local farms, distilled, aged, and bottled in West Virginia. The third series, Contradiction, is a mingling of their homemade whiskey and sourced whiskeys.

Drop by the beautiful tasting room, cozy up to the bar, and taste them all to find your favorite. Allow time for a distillery tour and look around the gift shop for other WV products, such as Holl's Chocolates infused with Smooth Ambler Bourbon.

745 Industrial Park Rd., Maxwelton 24957
(304) 497-3123, smoothambler.com

DINE
AT A NOSTALGIC CARHOP EATERY

It is true that everything in style circles back and becomes relevant again. But some things never go out of style, like carhop eateries where you order from the comfort of your vehicle and a server brings your food and drink out to you. West Virginia has quite a few nostalgic gems across the state, serving classic and comfort food dishes, shakes and malts, fries and onion rings, and specialty dishes.

Visiting Frostop Drive-In always makes me giddy with happiness. Frostop Drive-In even has little trays for your window track, adding a place to hold your order. These were the places poised for the quickest regain of visitors throughout the dreariest COVID times. Try the classic homemade root-beer float, and enjoy the throwback treat from the comfort of your car at this retro Huntington landmark with the giant frosty mug atop the roof.

1449 Hal Greer Blvd., Huntington 25701
(304) 523-6851
facebook.com/Frostop-Drive-In-165888996796186

OTHER EXQUISITE CARHOP EATERIES TO CONSIDER

Sterling Drive-In
788 Stewart St., Welch 24801
(304) 436-3271, facebook.com/pages/
Sterling-Drive-Inn/186102908068450

King Tut Drive-In
301 N Eisenhower Dr., Beckley 25801
(304) 252-6353, kingtutdrivein.com

Lynn's Drive Inn
3705 Coal Heritage Rd., Bluefield 24701
(304) 589-6279
facebook.com/profile.php?id=100057394362827

Burger Carte
175 Virginia Ave., Smithers 25186
(304) 442-2071, burgercartefoods.com

Morrison's Drive Inn
126 Stollings Ave., Logan 25601
(304) 752-9872, facebook.com/Morrisons-Drive-Inn-Offical-Site-114921678593024

Jim's Drive-In
479 Washington St., Lewisburg 24901
(304) 645-2590, facebook.com/jimsdrivein

FEAST
AT THYME BISTRO

If you find yourself in Lewis County, central West Virginia, look no further than Thyme Bistro for a fantastic meal. Thyme Bistro uses locally sourced meats and produce for its eclectic upscale menu. The menu options change seasonally to guarantee that guests get meals made from the freshest ingredients.

Start your dining experience with a bowl of homemade soup made fresh daily. Thyme Bistro's steaks are always tender and flavorful, and the filet mignon with whipped potatoes is one of the best things on the menu. Another popular item is the potato parmesan encrusted salmon with a side of spinach, tomato, and fontina cheese gratin. You will want to save room for dessert or take some to go. The house-made desserts are always amazing and the perfect finish to a delightful meal.

125 Main Ave., Weston 26452
(304) 269-7177, thyme-bistro.business.site

FILL UP
AT THE WONDER BAR STEAKHOUSE

The Wonder Bar Steakhouse in Clarksburg has served the finest steaks, seafood, chops, and pasta since 1946. You will feel as if you've stepped back in time to Supper Club days. Wonder Bar's hand-cut steaks and chops are aged and seasoned with a special seasoning blend that creates the basis for the best melt-in-your-mouth steaks. Imagine yourself with a tender filet mignon and a South African lobster tail—this isn't your average surf and turf! If you're looking for something lighter, you'll love the Mickster Salad.

The Wonder Bar has been awarded the *Wine Spectator*'s Award of Excellence for nine years because of its expansive wine selection. Dine in the newly updated dining room or enjoy the view from Wonder Bar's outdoor dining patio. Reservations are recommended; they are closed on Sundays.

1012 Wonderbar Rd., Clarksburg 26301
(304) 622-1451, wonderbarsteakhouse.com

SATISFY YOUR SWEET TOOTH
AT LOCAL PASTRY SHOPS

There are many places to delight your sweet tooth across the Mountain State. I remember strolling Capitol Street, circa the 1970s, with my mom, sampling cookies and cupcakes from local bakeries and then getting a bag of malted milk balls or salted cashews from the Peanut Shoppe, 126 Capitol Street. Today, you can still get a large selection of warm nuts (salted, unsalted, roasted, raw, and in the shell) and chocolates, seeds, dried fruit, and candies—including sugar-free. There is popcorn and fudge for the non-bagged candy consumer and oddball choices like licorice jelly beans, fruit sours, and French burnt peanuts.

Something special about the Peanut Shoppe is that they still use much of the original 1950s equipment. It's a glorious day when they are roasting peanuts in the shell, and the smells waft into the street, luring people in droves.

126 Capitol St., Charleston 25301
(304) 342-9493, peanutshoppewv.com

OTHER PLACES FOR TASTY TREATS AROUND WV

Almost Heaven Desserts & Coffee Shop
100 W Main St., Bridgeport 26330
(304) 848-2500, almostheavendesserts.com

Spring Hill Pastry Shop
600 Chestnut St., Charleston 25309
(304) 768-7397, springhillpastry.com

Nu-Era Bakery
120 Stratton St. #3611, Logan 25601
(304) 752-2033, facebook.com/nuerabakery

Quality Bake Shoppe
1004 Second St., Moundsville 26041
(304) 845-3452, facebook.com/qualitybakeshoppe

Paula Vega Cakes and Coffee Shop
308 9th St., Huntington 25701
(304) 972-2253, paulavegacakes.com

Royalicious
126 Patrick Henry Way
Charles Town 25414
(304) 728-4663, www.facebook.com/profile.php?id=100069835305083

CHANNEL YOUR INNER FOODIE
AT TASTE OF OUR TOWN

Taste of Our Town (TOOT) is one of Lewisburg's largest annual events, held in October. This event is organized by Carnegie Hall and brings in thousands of visitors each year. Visitors purchase tokens to buy food samples from local restaurants and vendors at the numerous tents around town.

The event is more than just food, though. Carnegie Hall has art exhibits, live music, and even artisans demonstrating their crafts, such as clay sculpting, basket weaving, and woodworking. The shops in Lewisburg and the Carnegie Hall Gallery are open for the event. Bring the children for a fun day of face painting, a stilt-walking balloon artist, live performances, and so much more. TOOT is a fun, family-friendly day for celebrating fall, food, and the arts.

611 Church St., Lewisburg 24901
(304) 645-7917, carnegiehallwv.org

DRINK A COLD ONE
AT PIES & PINTS

Pies & Pints is a great place to sip a cold one. Though they aren't in the beer-brewing business, you can choose from around 20 beers on tap, 30-plus cans, and 30 to 50 bottles at any of the three locations (Charleston, Fayetteville, and Morgantown). Pair your drink with the Pork & Pepper Nachos. The Grape & Gorgonzola is a specialty pizza that will rock your taste buds. Pies & Pints was purchased, franchised, and can currently be found at 14 locations across six states. Fayetteville remains with the original owners, where it originated.

If you are more into the craft beer scene, West Virginia has a robust number of breweries. With an extensive selection of pints and flights, you'll also find a fun and comfortable place to hang out, bring your pet and family, and enjoy the fun at Weathered Ground Brewery in Ghent.

Pies & Pints
222 Capitol St., Charleston 25301
(304) 342-7437

1002 Suncrest Towne Centre,
Morgantown 26505
(304) 777-4749

219 W Maple Ave.,
Fayetteville 25840
(304) 574-2200, piesandpints.net

Weathered Ground Brewery
2027 Flat Top Rd., Ghent 25843
(304) 223-2500
weatheredgroundbrewery.com

MORE PLACES FOR YOUR WV BREWERIES CRAWL—MANY OFFERING TOURS, FOOD, AND GROWLER REFILLS

Berkeley Springs Brewing Co.
110 Michigan Ln., Berkeley Springs 25411
(304) 258-3369
berkeleyspringsbrewingcompany.com

Screech Owl Brewing
2323 Ralph Livengood Rd., Bruceton Mills 26525
(304) 379-4777
screechowlbrewing.com

Abolitionist Ale Works
129 W Washington St., Charles Town 25414
(681) 252-1548, abolitionistaleworks.com

Bad Shepherd Brewery
702 Quarrier St., Charleston 25301
(304) 343-2739
blacksheepwv.com/charleston/
bad-shepherd-brewery

Stumptown Ales
390 William Ave., Davis 26260
(304) 259-5570
stumptownales.com

Big Timber Brewing Co.
1210 S Davis Ave., Elkins 26241
(304) 637-5008
bigtimberbrewing.com

Bridge Brew Works
335 Nick Rahall Greenway, Fayetteville 25840
(304) 574-4600
bridgebrewworks.com

Greenbrier Valley Brewing
862 Industrial Park Dr., Ste. A, Maxwelton 24957
(304) 520-4669
gvbc.beer

Parkersburg Brewing Co.
707 Market St., Parkersburg 26101
(304) 916-1502
parkersburgbrewing.com

Sophisticated Hound Brewing Co.
833 Mercer St., Princeton 24740
(304) 320-6674
facebook.com/sophisticatedhoundbrewing

High Ground Brewing
102 Railroad Ave., Terra Alta 26764
(304) 789-1216
highgroundbrewing.co

Mountain State Brewing Co.
One Nelson Blvd., Thomas 26292
(304) 463-4500
or
54 Clay St., Morgantown 26501
(304) 241-1976
mountainstatebrewing.com

GATHER WITH FRIENDS FOR FINE DINING
AT THE PRESS ROOM

Amid the main thoroughfare in downtown Shepherdstown lies the Press Room, a fine dining experience with a casual vibe, outstanding imported oysters, fine wines, and impeccable service. The site is a circa-1793 former newspaper building with a classy interior, exposed brick walls, and a rich appearance. Guests are treated to complimentary bread and dipping oil while choosing menu options, which change seasonally.

The Press Room's fare ranges from grilled rib eyes with gorgonzola butter to soft-shell crab when in season. The house pâté should not be missed, but save room for dessert. These include a light and luscious panna cotta with fresh berries and fig vincotto, a zabaglione, and an incredible creme brûlée. This is a memorable dinner, no matter what the reason is that brings you. Reservations are recommended.

129 W German St., Shepherdstown 25443
(304) 876-8777, pressroomwv.com

STAY
IN A EUROPEAN-REMINISCENT INN

The beautiful historic town of Shepherdstown is one of West Virginia's finest treasures. The Bavarian Inn, offering luxury chalet, standard, and manor rooms, draws tourists from all over because of its European charm and grace. Chalet rooms have balconies overlooking the river, while the manor view offers gas fireplaces and whirlpool tubs. Standard rooms have a cozy sitting area for relaxing.

Not to be missed is the gorgeous infinity pool overlooking the Potomac River, a popular spot (weather permitting) for enjoying cocktails and food. Bavarian Inn is also known for its gourmet dining, often with locally sourced ingredients, in a gorgeous dining room with a German flair. Whether you are dining in the prestigious Potomac Room or the Pub Room patio, it is sure to please.

164 Shepherd Grade Rd., Shepherdstown 25443
(304) 876-2551, bavarianinnwv.com

TIP
Check out the onsite brewery, too—Bavarian Brothers Brewing.

Camden Park

MUSIC AND ENTERTAINMENT

SECURE YOUR TICKET
TO THE WEST VIRGINIA STATE FAIR

The State Fair of West Virginia, a nearly 100-year-old tradition, runs in Lewisburg for ten days each August. It offers Junior 4H, FFA livestock and horse shows, draft horse pulls, world-class concerts, rides, and everybody's favorite: fair food. State fair attractions range from farm equipment to gorgeous handblown glassware, all made in West Virginia. There are long-standing traditions at the WV State Fair, like the Ben-Ellen Donuts, started in 1952. Nothing compares to these deep-fried cinnamon sugarcoated donuts, sold only during the fair. The lines are long, but the donuts are worth the wait. The barns are also a popular draw, filled with pigs, cows, sheep, llamas, and horses. If you are patient, you might see a calf being born in the birthing tent.

947 Maplewood Ave., Lewisburg 24902
(304) 645-1090, statefairofwv.com

LISTEN
TO GREAT LIVE MUSIC IN THOMAS

The Purple Fiddle is a family-friendly, music lovers' paradise. Live music is the mainstay of this popular nonsmoking hot spot tucked away in Thomas, a beautiful Allegheny Mountains town in Tucker County. Purple Fiddle keeps the ticket prices very reasonable, making them easily accessible. They offer a live show on Friday and Saturday nights, with music ranging from rock 'n' roll to Celtic, reggae, and jazz.

Along with a big selection of local and imported beers, IPAs, and wines, the Purple Fiddle's menu is loaded with freshly made sandwiches and wraps for enjoying while listening to music, and the homemade hummus and salsa are not to be missed. While waiting for the music to start, walk along the main street and browse the quaint shops for antiques, books, toys, and even a Christmas Shoppe.

96 East Ave., Thomas 26292
(304) 463-4040, purplefiddle.com

RELAX AFTER WORK
AT HADDAD RIVERFRONT PARK

Haddad Riverfront Park is Charleston's entertainment hub. Sitting on the banks of the Kanawha River, this venue was built in the 1980s to host concerts, live events, and the Sternwheel Regatta. The main stage (Schoenbaum Stage) and retractable canopy were gifts from the state's biggest benefactor, Betty Schoenbaum. It is surrounded by a 2,500-seat amphitheater and is the West Virginia Symphony's primary home.

It also hosts seasonal fireworks, chili cook-offs, and the levee's car shows. The free Live on the Levee concert series runs Memorial Day weekend through Labor Day weekend. Boaters can dock at the floating boat dock on the levee for a primo seat.

Though the Charleston Sternwheel Regatta took a 14-year hiatus, it was back in June 2022, bigger and better than ever. The locals are so thrilled to have their premier festival reborn.

600 Kanawha Blvd. E, Charleston 25301
(304) 348-6860 charlestonwv.com/listing/haddad-riverfront-park
and charlestonregatta.com

ENCOUNTER THE UNIMAGINABLE
AT TALA

Trans-Allegheny Lunatic Asylum (TALA) in Weston offers the creepiest site in West Virginia. TALA was originally the Weston State Hospital in operation from 1864 to 1994 and served as a sanctuary for the mentally ill. It was here that more lobotomies were performed than anywhere else. People died there; torture was evident. The ghosts of previous residents and children born at the hospital wander the halls, making TALA one of the most haunted places in America.

Don't believe me? Learn more about this National Historic Landmark by watching the numerous TV shows recorded there, including *Paranormal Lockdown*, Travel Channel's *Destination Fear*, and Syfy's *Ghost Hunters*. Besides the psychiatric hospital history, this massive limestone structure also has intriguing tales of Civil War raids and more. Historic Civil War, Cemetery and Farm, Asylum after Dark, and Paranormal tours are given daily, Tuesday through Sunday.

71 Asylum Dr., Weston 26452
(304) 269-5070, trans-alleghenylunaticasylum.com

TRY YOUR HAND
AT BINGO

The Dunbar Bingo Hall offers stellar gaming and is also a social event. Bingo runs Saturday afternoon through evening to a packed house. Besides a few hours of bingo (regular games, quickies, and early birds), they also sell $1 tips at this bingo. If you've never experienced opening tips to see if you won an instant prize or holding a "tip" toward a larger seal prize, I recommend it. I may be the fastest tip opener in history.

The Dunbar Bingo Hall allows you to bring in your own food and drink, or you can enjoy a great selection of foods and desserts, mostly homemade, from the concession stand. The staff is friendly, the vibe is energetic, and it's an all-around good time. Dunbar Athletic Boosters, a nonprofit organization, runs the bingo through a volunteer network. Proceeds benefit the local area schools and extracurricular activities.

2605 Charles Ave., Dunbar 25064
(304) 768-5156

SIT UNDER THE STARS
FOR A PERFORMANCE

Grandview Theater, now known as Theatre West Virginia, is a delightful way to experience a first-class stage show performed in an outdoor setting under the stars. Theatre West Virginia has stage shows, concerts, and drama and theater camps.

Rocket Boys: The Musical, based on West Virginia native Homer Hickam's best-selling memoir, and *Hatfields and McCoys* are two of the most popular shows. The long-running *Hatfields and McCoys* (I mean, I saw it as a child almost 50 years ago) is a special thing to experience at Theatre West Virginia. It is the story of two Appalachian mountaineer families engaged in a legendary feud attracting mega attention in the late 1800s.

4700 Grandview Rd., Beaver 25813
(304) 256-6800, theatrewestvirginia.org

DID YOU KNOW?

This story became world-famous when Kevin Costner (accompanied by a star-studded cast) starred in and coproduced the three-part Emmy Award–winning miniseries and dramatization based on the Hatfields and McCoys in 2012.

PLAY OR ROCK OUT
AT THE CLAY CENTER

One of the country's most unique facilities is the Clay Center in Charleston. It is three separate venues, all housed in a 240,000-square-foot property dedicated to music, art, science, and theater. This hub of culture offers the Avampato Discovery Museum, a three-floor museum with interactive family-friendly exhibits; the Caperton Planetarium & Theater (state-of-the-art Electric Sky); and the Juliet Art Museum. The Discovery Museum has Ashton's Climbing Sculpture, a kid-sized version of Charleston with various shops and services, and a WaterWorks play area.

Not to miss at the Clay Center are the world-class concerts and Broadway shows at Maier Foundation Performance Hall, also home to the fantastic West Virginia Symphony.

One Clay Sq., Charleston 25301
(304) 561-3570, theclaycenter.org

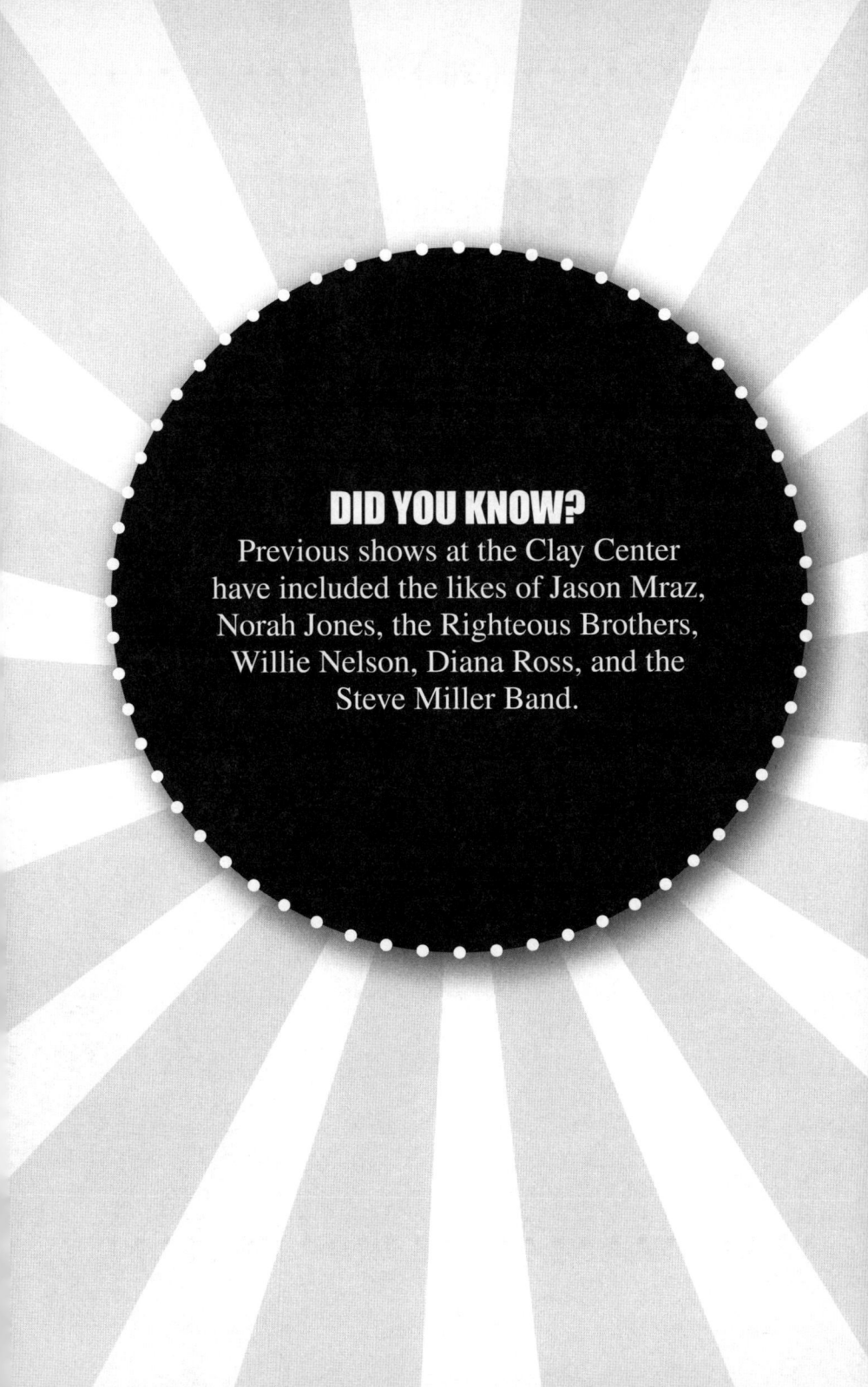

DID YOU KNOW?
Previous shows at the Clay Center have included the likes of Jason Mraz, Norah Jones, the Righteous Brothers, Willie Nelson, Diana Ross, and the Steve Miller Band.

REMINISCE
AT CAMDEN PARK

Enjoy family fun at the "Sign of the Happy Clown" west of Huntington in Wayne County near the Ohio–West Virginia border. Camden Park has been entertaining West Virginians and tristate residents for generations. Billed as a nostalgic attraction, it is one of only 13 trolley parks still open in the country. You'll enjoy all the fun of an older theme park with old-fashioned midway games, carnival-style eats, and eight kiddie rides. Semi–thrill rides include the Rattler, Kite Flyer, and the Paratrooper. Camden Park also has a retro haunted house and Skyliner, an aerial observation ride.

There aren't many places where you can still ride a 100-plus-year-old wooden roller coaster (the Big Dipper) or the soaking log flume. Be sure to eat a classic Pronto Pup corn dog, a Camden Park tradition. Add-on activities include Swan Lake paddleboats and mini golf. Camden Park is open from May through October. There is a parking fee.

5000 Waverly Rd., Huntington 25704
(304) 429-4321, camdenpark.com

UNCOVER WV'S QUIRKIEST ATTRACTION:
THE MYSTERY HOLE

The Mystery Hole has long been a favorite roadside attraction on US-60 in Ansted. This one-of-a-kind find will impress your friends and family and makes for a great stopping point on a leaf-peeping or scenic road trip. The Mystery Hole is a gravity-defying wonder. You'll be baffled by seeing water run uphill and a chair lifted into the air and set against a wall that can hold a grown adult's weight just by gravity alone.

Fifteen-minute guided tours of this quirky, interesting attraction run $10 for adults (prices may change) on Fridays, Saturdays, and Sundays. Infants and pets are not allowed.

16724 Midland Trail, Ansted 25812
(304) 658-9101, mysteryhole.com

TIP
The Mystery Hole is 15 minutes from the New River Gorge Bridge, also a national park. It's an easy drive to add a second phenomenal sight in the Mountain State.

PROWL AROUND
AT HOVATTER'S WILDLIFE ZOO

From April to October, and on weekends in November, you can enjoy seeing and meeting the hundreds of animals at Hovatter's Wildlife Zoo (the West Virginia Zoo) in Kingwood, Preston County. The wildlife zoo is just off WV-7 and has easy access from the parking lot to the zoo attractions. Native and exotic animals you can see at Hovatter's include tigers, lemurs, chimpanzees, grizzly bears, wild boars, capuchin monkeys, giraffes, and much more.

Admission runs $12.99 for adults and $10.99 for children ages 3 to 12. You can also buy food in the gift shop to hand-feed many of the animals, and the zoo even has signs posted at each animal exhibit letting you now what kind of food is allowed. Hovatter's Wildlife Zoo has been operating in Preston County since 1993.

291 Wagner Ln., Kingwood 26537
(304) 329-3122, westvirginiazoo.com

TIP
If you have trouble walking or if it is sweltering, plan what you want to see before starting your zoo trek.

ATTEND
A MOUNTAIN STAGE CONCERT

Since 1983, the Mountain Stage music radio show has been recorded live in Charleston. Singer-songwriter Larry Groce helped create the show, which is broadcast by West Virginia Public Broadcasting and distributed by NPR, and it has since gone on to host musical artists like Bruce Hornsby, Peter Buck, Natalie Merchant, and Norah Jones. Groce worked as both the show's host and artistic director until he retired in 2021, passing his hosting duties off to country music star and West Virginia native Kathy Mattea.

You can catch a two-hour live show at the Culture Center Theater in the West Virginia State Museum. Guests range from seasoned greats to emerging stars, and the music is always impressive. Tickets run $25 online and $30 at the door on the show date if available.

1900 Kanawha Blvd E, Charleston 25311
(304) 558-0220, mountainstage.org

JOURNEY THROUGH
ORGAN CAVE

With 45 miles of mapped trails, Organ Cave has the distinguished titles of National Historic and National Natural Landmarks. It is also on the West Virginia Civil War Trail. Soldiers under the command of General Robert E. Lee mined for saltpeter from 1862–1865 to make gunpowder. Another notable find from the cave was the first prehistoric three-toed sloth discovered in the late 1700s. Guests can take a guided walking tour to learn more about the cave's collection of stalagmites and stalactites. You won't want to miss seeing the 90-foot underground waterfall in the Chapel Room as well as the large rock formation that resembles a large organ from which the town and cave got their names. If you are a bit more adventurous, you can tour the cave depths in a Wild Caving tour.

242 Organ Cave Dr., Ronceverte 24970
(304) 645-7600, organcave.com

31

TREAT YOURSELF
TO A SALT SPA EXPERIENCE

A unique experience that you do not want to miss is Pomona Salt Cave and Spa. The owners created an artificial cave into the side of a mountain in the gorgeous Greenbrier Valley with over 18,000 pounds of imported Himalayan sea salt from the floor to the ceiling. The hand-painted decor sets an ambiance of pure relaxation.

Sit in a relaxing chair after stepping in and walking across the salt bed, and you'll feel the weight of the world easing from your shoulders. The halotherapy session is 45 minutes of relaxation and soothing music to complete the experience. Next door to the cave is Pomona Spa, offering various spa treatments for couples and singles. They have a café, too, so you can plan a whole day of pampering. Also on the property is a small lodge perfect for small groups.

6705 Pocahontas Trail, White Sulfur Springs 24986
(304) 536-2222, thesaltcaveandspa.com

32

PLACE YOUR WAGER
IN CHARLES TOWN

Experience live thoroughbred horse racing in Charles Town, less than an hour from the bigger cities of Baltimore and Washington, DC. Hollywood Casino at Charles Town Races is where to go for horse racing and every state-of-the-art thing associated with the casino world. The well-appointed casino, with all the bells and whistles that rival the ones in Las Vegas, offers 184,000 square feet of gambling space and nearly 2,000 slots. Table games (74 currently) range from mini-baccarat and blackjack to pai gow poker and Mississippi stud. Craps, roulette, and electronic table games are also big draws. Hollywood Casino bills top-name concert headliners and shows and offers various restaurants to fit your budget.

Its most well-known races include Race for the Ribbon, Charles Town Classic, and the West Virginia Breeders Classics. There is also simulcast horse and dog racing.

750 Hollywood Dr., Charles Town 25414
(800) 795-7001, hollywoodcasinocharlestown.com

TIP
Make it an overnight with a choice of hotel rooms and suites at the pristine property.

Droop Mountain
Lookout Tower

SPORTS AND RECREATION

TEE UP
AT THE BEST WV GOLF COURSES

West Virginia is among the highest-rated places for golfers on the East Coast. The Greenbrier is synonymous with world-class golfing, offering three top-rated, picturesque resort courses: the Greenbrier, the Old White, and the Meadows. Old White was the Greenbrier's first 18-hole golf course, which opened in 1914. The Greenbrier Course is the only one in the world to have hosted both the Ryder Cup and Solheim Cup. Jack Nicklaus redesigned the course in the 1970s. The Greenbrier's newest golf offering is a nine-hole walking course, Ashford Short, perfect for those who don't have enough time for a full round. And lastly, there is a private course rated among America's elite.

Most golf legends have played here, including Tiger Woods, Bubba Watson, Arnold Palmer, and Phil Mickelson. You can also take lessons from the Greenbrier's pros.

101 Main St. W, White Sulphur Springs 24986
(855) 453-4858, greenbrier.com/golf

OTHER PLACES TO GET YOUR GOLF GAME ON

Glade Springs Resort Golf Course

Cobb Course at Glade Springs features 51 sand bunkers, 200 feet of elevation fluctuation, slopes, shifting sun angles, and eight lakes. The Cobb Course has welcomed the West Virginia Open and NCAA National Championship, and has been a qualifier for the US Open. Come in April and October for the best rates.

255 Resort Dr., Daniels 25832
(304) 763-2000, gladesprings.com/golf

Pete Dye Golf Club

The Pete Dye Golf Club can boast being number 87 on *Golf Digest*'s Ranking of America's 100 Greatest Courses, but the true accolade goes to Pete Dye himself for transforming a former 250-acre Appalachian Mountain coal mine into one of the greatest works of his career. The "course that tempts and tests you from the opening tee shot to your final putt" is a golfer's dream.

801 Aaron Smith Dr., Bridgeport 26330
(304) 842-2801, petedye.com

Twisted Gun Golf Club

Another links-style 18-hole golf course created on a former coal mine in Mingo County, Twisted Gun has four sets of tees, plays 7,105 yards from the professional tees, and has hosted the WVGA Senior Four-Ball Championship and regional qualifiers for the West Virginia Open and Mid-amateur. They welcome all skill levels.

2002 Twisted Gun Rd., Wharncliffe 25651
(304) 687-1514, facebook.com/twistedgungolfclub

34

WITNESS WV'S
ONLY NATIONAL PARK

Come prepared for your New River Gorge National Park and Preserve hike with plenty of water and hiking shoes, as you will come across several steep spots along the way. The open cliff edge at the end of the trail is a gorgeous spot to sit, take in the views of the bridge and the Appalachian Mountains, and rest up in the shade for the hike back. See why our state's beloved tagline, Almost Heaven, is so appropriate.

The New River Gorge is one of the newest additions to the National Park Service roster. One of the best views of the iconic New River Gorge Bridge can be seen at the end of Long Point Trail in Fayetteville. This roughly three-mile round-trip hike is labeled moderate difficulty, so consider that when planning your trip.

Follow WV-16 to Gatewood Road and follow the signs.
(304) 465-0508, nps.gov/neri

TIP
To get your passport stamped, stop in the Canyon Rim Visitor Center.

PICNIC
AT COOPERS ROCK STATE FOREST

Coopers Rock State Forest in Bruceton Mills is a charming spot to hike, bike (50 miles of trails), and enjoy a picnic lunch at one of the many covered spots (complete with grills, drinking water, and a restroom). Coopers Rock is about 13 miles from Morgantown. The epic property offers an overlook above the Cheat River Gorge, the icing on the cake. There is even cell service for a quick Facebook Live to share your stunning sandstone cliff scenery with friends and family. Coopers Rock is a perfect destination to experience the rhododendron, West Virginia's state flower, as the sheer number of them is incredible.

You will also see the remains of the Henry Clay Furnace at Coopers Rock State Forest, the first steam-powered blast furnace in the surrounding area. Popular activities at the state forest are bouldering, cross-country skiing, and trout fishing.

61 County Line Dr., Bruceton Mills 26525
(304) 594-1561, wvstateparks.com/park/coopers-rock-state-forest

SIT COURTSIDE
AT A WVU BASKETBALL GAME

West Virginia University may be the pride of the Mountain State, but the thrill of watching a basketball game courtside in the WVU Coliseum may be the hottest ticket in Morgantown.

The West Virginia Mountaineers men's basketball team—the blue and gold—is a member of the Big 12 Conference in the NCAA Division led by Hall of Fame recipient Head Coach Bob Huggins, Huggy Bear to many. The team has earned the nickname "Press Virginia" due to their outstanding defense on the court. Since becoming head coach, Bob Huggins has worked hard to instill a sense of community and appreciation of the WV fanbase in his players. The players participate in many community events to give back to the fans and thank them for their support.

West Virginia Coliseum
3450 Monongahela Blvd., Morgantown 26505
(800) 988-4263, wvusports.com

DID YOU KNOW?
The West Virginia Mountaineers have been to the Final Four twice, in 2010 and in 1959 with legendary player Jerry West.

COZY INTO A CABIN
AT THE ASHLAND RESORT

Whether you are exploring West Virginia for the Hatfield-McCoy Trail System or otherwise, Ashland Resort in Northfork is a stellar place to rest your head. Nestled among a beautiful hardwood forest, this little slice of heaven offers a 1,600-acre camping facility with RV spots, cozy cabins, retreat houses, cottages, and tent sites. The cottages and cabins are styled with rustic features, TVs, kitchenettes, and comfortable sleeping accommodations. Fire rings, picnic tables, and porch swings add to the homeyness and allure of this beautiful setting.

Ashland Resort also has a camp store, with goods ranging from souvenirs and firewood to frozen and fresh food, drinks, and candy. The resort has direct access to the Indian Ridge Trail.

246 Totem Pole Rd., Northfork 24868
(304) 862-2322, atvresort.com

DID YOU KNOW?
Ashland Resort has handicap-accessible park model RVs for rent.

PLUNGE WEST VIRGINIA'S
IMPRESSIVE WHITEWATER RAPIDS

Whitewater rafting is one of the most popular and well-known activities that attract people from all over the world. The New and Gauley rivers are famous waterways where you can raft in wild, wonderful West Virginia.

Adventures on the Gorge is the premier whitewater rafting outfitter, offering a variety of packages that cater to your skill level. The New River is perfect for all skill levels, while the Gauley is geared more toward the experienced. Rafting season runs spring to fall, with packages ranging from a half or full day to even an overnight stay with two days of rafting excitement. They have restaurants and a pub to relax in after your long day on the river.

219 Chestnutburg Rd., Lansing 25862
(855) 379-8738, adventuresonthegorge.com

DID YOU KNOW?
No experience is necessary—your qualified guide will show you the ropes and deliver the thrill of a lifetime.

TAKE
A SCENIC TRAIN RIDE IN ELKINS

The newly desirable scenic train travel trips are not new to West Virginia. For years, we've had Cass Scenic Railroad and Potomac Eagle riding the rails for riders to enjoy the majestic Mountain State. There are two locations where you can hop aboard a train or steam locomotive journey to access scenic points of interest. Many will get you up close and personal with jaw-dropping scenery.

The Tygart Railroad Flyer at the Durbin & Greenbrier Valley Railroad is one of the newest offerings at the Elkins Depot, running April through November. The four-hour vintage diesel-powered train ride takes you to see a gorgeous waterfall (at the High Falls of Cheat) through an S-curve tunnel and high bridge. It is a fun and memorable experience; take the whole family.

315 Railroad Ave., Elkins 26241
(304) 636-9477, mountainrailwv.com

TIP
Some of the climate-controlled train cars offer a buffet-style lunch; I recommend the Parlor Car.

GIVE ROCK CLIMBING A CHANCE
AT SENECA ROCKS

West Virginia has countless trails from easy to extreme terrain, so there is something for everyone to enjoy, including families. One of West Virginia's most iconic sites is Seneca Rocks in Pendleton County. It is a popular site for experienced rock climbers to traverse the near-vertical front side of the rocks. Not to worry, you can still enjoy the view from the top by taking in the hiking path designed to allow anyone to walk up to the observation deck.

At the base of the rocks is a visitor center with an indoor rock wall for climbing and many art displays. It is a great place to learn about Seneca Rocks' formations and the surrounding area. The homestead cabin built in 1839 shows off the craftsmanship that went into creating the cabin with locally sourced materials of the time.

Junction of US 33, WV 28, and WV 55, Seneca Rocks 26884
(304) 567-2827, fs.usda.gov/recarea/mnf/recarea/?recid=7051

TIP
The view from the top is well worth the climb.

Seneca Rocks

GO STARGAZING
IN HILLSBORO

West Virginia has some of the best stargazing spots on the entire East Coast, away from the light pollution of big cities and high-traffic areas. Partake in stargazing at Droop Mountain Battlefield State Park (one of West Virginia's least-populated areas) in Hillsboro, Pocahontas County.

Droop Mountain Battlefield State Park's lookout tower, nearby Watoga State Park (a designated International Dark Sky Park), and Calvin Price State Forest have coordinated their Dark Sky programming and activities. They have hosted star parties to attract visitors and share its stellar location. Star parties are complete with an astronomer and a telescope to allow visitors an opportunity to see the moon and visible planets. You can find the dates on their website. Droop Mountain Battlefield State Park is also on the Civil War Discovery Trail.

Droop Mountain Battlefield State Park
683 Droop Park Rd.,
Hillsboro 24946
(304) 653-4254, wvstateparks.com/park/droop-mountain-battlefield-state-park

Watoga State Park
4800 Watoga Park Rd.,
Marlinton 24954
(304) 799-4087, wvstateparks.com/park/watoga-state-park

TIP
Bring your camera for some amazing pictures of the Milky Way.

MORE PLACES TO STARE AT STARS IN WV

Blackwater Falls State Park
1584 Blackwater Lodge Rd., Davis 26260
(304) 259-5216
wvstateparks.com/park/blackwater-falls-state-park

Lost River State Park
Lost River is one of the most remote state parks in West Virginia.

321 Park Dr., Mathias 26812
(304) 897-5372
wvstateparks.com/park/lost-river-state-park

Cranny Crow, at Lost River in Hardy County, is one of the only stargazing destinations where you can see the Milky Way rise over five counties in two states. Accommodations at this property include comfy cabins and Tentrr campsites.

Seneca State Forest
Seneca State Forest's 65-foot Thorny Mountain Fire Tower offers unobstructed night sky views above the tree-laden forest.

10135 Browns Creek Rd., Dunmore 24934
(304) 799-6213
wvstateparks.com/park/seneca-state-forest

CHANT "WE ARE MARSHALL" AT A HOME GAME

The Thundering Herd, an intercollegiate varsity sports program of Marshall University, plays at the Joan C. Edwards Stadium in Huntington. With a sea of green, you can cheer Marshall University's college football team on to victory, along with a loyal and devout following. There is inexplicable energy in the air, and even if you don't care for football, I can't imagine anyone having anything other than a great time. Marshall's past greats include Randy Moss, Byron Leftwich, Carl Lee, and Chad Pennington.

An unfortunate Southern Airways plane crash in 1970, carrying 37 members of the Herd football team, eight coaching staff, 25 boosters, and five airline personnel, left 75 dead. A 2006 major motion picture, *We Are Marshall* starring Matthew McConaughey, depicted and memorialized the tragic true-story event, which we West Virginians never forget.

2001 Third Ave., Huntington 25703
(304) 696-3170, herdzone.com

WATCH MARSHALL UNIVERSITY AND OTHER COLLEGE AND PRO SPORTS AT THESE POPULAR SPORTS BARS, WITH GREAT FOOD AND DRINKS TO BOOT.

Adelphia Sports Bar & Grille
218 Capitol St., Charleston 25301
(304) 343-5551, adelphiasportsbar.com

Kegler's Sports Bar & Grille
735-A Chestnut Ridge Rd., Morgantown 26505
(304) 598-9698, keglerssportsbar.com

JP Henry's
5106 Emerson Ave., Parkersburg 26104
(304) 485-9390, facebook.com/j.p.henrysrestaurant

Basil's Sports Bar & Grill
27 Marshaling Yard Dr., Weirton 26062
(304) 914-4478, basilssportsbar.com

TJ's Sports Garden Restaurant
808 National Rd., Wheeling 26003
(304) 232-9555, tjswheeling.com

SMELL THE ROSES
AT RITTER PARK

The Ritter Park Rose Garden, created in the 1930s, is a free point of interest at the Ritter Park in Huntington. Manicured gardens with around three thousand roses, all well labeled, occupy a portion of the park, including an event space and reception area. The nationally recognized Ritter Park Rose Garden is one of the most beautiful in the state. All-American rose selections are perfect for photographing. It is also an ideal place to familiarize yourself with rose varieties and learn while you admire them. Watch for full bloom status in late May to mid-June, with vivid and muted colors of red, yellow, white, purple, orange, and pink.

The Ritter Park Rose Garden, on Huntington's Southside, has become a popular wedding spot. Also at the park are tennis courts, a dog park, a walking trail, and an award-winning playground.

1570 McCoy Rd., Huntington 25701
(304) 696-5954, ghprd.org/index.php/rose-garden

SLEEP OUTDOORS
AT WATOGA

Camping is a wonderful way of getting out and truly enjoying the natural beauty of our state. West Virginia has many options for camping, depending on your style, from glamping to primitive.

Watoga State Park is my favorite of the state parks. This park has two campgrounds, Beaver Creek and Riverside. Riverside offers 38 units and electric hookups adjacent to the Greenbrier River (for boating and fishing), while Beaver Creek sits on the edge of the park and is a little quieter. Watoga State Park also rents cabins if that is your idea of roughing it. Amenities include a play area for kids, horse stables and trail rides, and a swimming pool. You will likely encounter lots of wildlife as you visit the park, so keep an eye out for deer, bears, and many others.

4800 Watoga Park Rd., Marlinton 24954
(304) 799-4087, wvstateparks.com/park/watoga-state-park

HIT THE SLOPES
AT SNOWSHOE

Snowshoe Mountain Resort is an ideal four-season mountain destination for families and adrenaline junkies alike! Snowshoe is known for winter sports (skiing, snowboarding, snow tubing, and snowmobiling), but in recent years, its mountain trails have been transformed into a world-class bike park (IMBA Ride Center), open May to October. The Mercedes-Benz UCI Mountain Bike World Cup will bring thousands of mountain bike enthusiasts worldwide to the Allegheny Mountains of Pocahontas County for the race weekend in September 2023.

Snowshoe's warmer months are great for taking a scenic chairlift to Shavers Lake beach for swimming, stand-up paddleboarding, inflatables, and kayaking, all included with the price of your lift ticket. You can also enjoy golfing at Raven Golf Course, e-bike tours, horseback riding, RZR and Segway tours, or Split Rock Pools. Snowshoe Mountain offers lodging choices, from a cozy room at the inn to the luxurious cabins and everything in between.

10 Snowshoe Dr., Snowshoe 26209
(877) 441-4386, snowshoemtn.com

CELEBRATE THE HOLIDAY SPIRIT
AT OGLEBAY RESORT

Oglebay Resort is a gorgeous park in the rolling hills outside of Wheeling. Lodging options are rooms in the rustic Wilson Lodge as well as two- to eight-bedroom cottages. Summer activities are endless, such as golfing on the championship courses designed by famed golfers Arnold Palmer and Robert Trent Jones, Sr., swimming in the Olympic-size pool, or, if you'd prefer, relaxing in the afternoon or having an indulgent spa treatment.

Mansion Museum offers shopping, various dining options, and the Bissonnette Gardens, particularly gorgeous in the spring. The Good Zoo has more than 50 animals on exhibit, with many endangered or protected species. The winter months at Oglebay Resort are extraordinary, beginning with the Festival of Lights, one of the nation's largest holiday light shows, which runs from November 10 to January 8. Skiing and snowboarding are also popular.

465 Lodge Dr., Wheeling 26003
(877) 436-1797, oglebay.com

FLOAT ON DOWN THE RIVER
IN ST. ALBANS

West Virginia has many mountain lakes and slow-moving rivers that are perfect for kayaking. It is a recreational sport that is easy for all ages and skill levels to partake in. Summer weekends have become prime time for floating trips, such as the Tour de Coal, which is the largest floating event in the state.

Tour de Coal takes place on the Coal River near St. Albans, on the outskirts of Charleston. In 2022, there were over 1,000 paddlers who dropped in to float. This event was in conjunction with Yak Fest, a street fair with live music, food, and vendors for all things kayaking. The Cheat River Water Trail spans 40 miles with nine access points and is considered a trail for boats, so rest your feet and grab a paddle.

Coal River Group
181 Pettigrew Ln., Tornado 25202
(304) 722-3055, coalrivergroup.com

RIDE
THE HATFIELD-MCCOY TRAIL SYSTEM

Southern West Virginia offers some of the hottest and newest West Virginia offerings. This pure Appalachian experience takes you into our world of magnificent outdoor offerings as you ride ATVs through the jaw-dropping off-highway vehicle trails' scenery. The Hatfield-McCoy Trails (HMT) allow you to hit the trails and see areas not typically open to the public on a high-thrills activity suited for the beginner or expert driver.

HMT is a multicounty project with facilities and trails in Boone, Kanawha, Lincoln, Logan, McDowell, Mercer, Mingo, Wayne, and Wyoming counties. It attracts visitors from all states and many countries from around the world. Trails range from beginner to expert, and one annual pass gets you onto every course in the system. Come soak up the scenery, go mudding, or blaze through the creeks and over mountain ranges of this bit of trail heaven, USA.

180 Appalachian Outpost Trail, Man 25635
(304) 752-3255, trailsheaven.com

EXPERIENCE THESE HATFIELD-MCCOY TRAILS

Ivy Branch (Lincoln Co.)
Can be used for full-size off-road vehicles like Land Cruisers and Jeeps

Bearwallow (Logan Co.)
One of the original HMT trails and most difficult

Rockhouse (Logan Co.)
One of the original HMT trails and highest difficulty; also largest single-trail system

Pocahontas (Mercer Co.)
The most continuous miles of trails east of the Mississippi

Indian Ridge (Mercer Co.)
Connects with three other HMT trails and for all difficulty levels

Buffalo Mountain (Mingo Co.)
The most historic trail in the system and most single-track trails

Devil Anse (Mingo Co.)
Located in the town of Matewan, the heart of the Hatfield and McCoy feud; connects to two other HMT systems and Buffalo Mountain for a total of 300-plus miles

Cabwaylingo State Forest (Wayne Co.)
Spans four counties

Pinnacle Creek (Wyoming Co.)
Breathtaking scenery and connects with three other HMT trails

Warrior (Wyoming Co.)
In WV's southernmost city and accesses the ATV-friendly city of Gary

SPLASH AROUND
SUMMERSVILLE LAKE

Camping is primo at Summersville Lake in Nicholas County. Whether you prefer a tent, cabin, RV camping, or boating, there is fun for the whole family at this beloved summer attraction with nearly 60 miles of shoreline. Summersville Lake is almost 400 feet deep, with stunning rock walls extending from the water to the heavens, providing a dramatic and photogenic setting. Tubing, jet skiing, and kayaking are just some things you can enjoy during your camping experience. Fishing is popular at Summersville Lake for catfish, walleye, bass, perch, and trout. The more quiet coves are the best places for hooking your catch.

If you've ever wanted to get scuba certified, you can do it at Summersville Lake.

2981 Summersville Lake Rd., Summersville 26651
(304) 872-3459, recreation.gov/camping/campgrounds/233422

TIP
Book your stay at Battle Run Campground, the campground on the shores of Summersville Lake, six months or so in advance.

… … … … … … (50) … … … … … …

PEDAL
A RECYCLED RAILWAY LINE

The concept of upcycling a retired railway line into a hiking and biking trail was genius, and the benefits are endless. Since railways were relatively flat, the courses were perfect for biking.

There are more than 60 rail trails in West Virginia. The popular Greenbrier River Trail is approximately 78 miles from Cass (near Snowshoe Resort) in Pocahontas County to Caldwell in Greenbrier County. It runs parallel to the gorgeous Greenbrier River and intercepts several small towns where bikers love to stop for breaks or overnights. There are break sites along the way where bikers are welcome to camp. Tunnels and bridges along the trail add to the epic scenic views you'll enjoy along the way. Another popular trail is the Blackwater Canyon Trail, which runs 10.5 miles. This trail is a bit more challenging since there are some inclines, but the waterfalls and gorgeous scenery make it all worthwhile.

4800 Watoga Park Rd., Marlinton 24954
(304) 799-4087, wvrailtrails.org

HAVE A FANTASTIC STAY
AT STONEWALL RESORT

Stonewall Resort is one of the most gorgeous, relaxing, and best places to stay, with 1,900 acres nestled around Stonewall Jackson Lake in Roanoke. It is also a state park with many green initiatives, a fantastic spa, great restaurants, and an Arnold Palmer Signature golf course.

Accommodations range from the Catskills of New York–looking main lodge to the secluded lakeside cottages and houses. There are ADA-accessible rooms, a lakeside campground (RVs and tents), and some pet-friendly (dogs and cats only) rooms. Amenities include hiking, biking, and 26 miles of shoreline for boating, fishing, swimming, and kayaking. There are also heated indoor and outdoor swimming pools and hot tubs, but the community fire pit and nightly s'mores-making is where the action is. Stillwaters is excellent for breakfast, lunch, and dinner, offering themed weekend buffets. They pride themselves on sourcing local fish, game, and produce.

940 Resort Dr., Roanoke 26447
(304) 269-7400, stonewallresort.com

FIND YOUR INNER THRILL SEEKER
AT ACE ADVENTURE RESORT

There is no better way to beat the summer heat than swimming in a cool spring-fed lake. Add dozens of inflatables to the five-acre water's playground, and you've reached the pinnacle of fun in the sun, or what Ace Adventure Resort has created. They even have their own beach. Their arsenal of inflatables features waterslides, trampolines, spinning Saturn balls, climbing walls that resemble small floating mountains, and even the famous BLOB!

Soar through the air and zip-line to the other side of the lake from the top of the tower. Dining options are also available at the lake, such as tasty wood-fired pizza from Woody's Grill. If you would like to plan a fun weekend, ACE Adventure Resort has cabins and camping accommodations available.

One Concho Rd., Oak Hill 25901
(800) 787-3982, aceraft.com

FISH
AT BLUESTONE LAKE

Go bass fishing at Bluestone Lake in Summers County, also noteworthy for catfish and trout. Though the scenic lake is a natural beauty, the outdoor offerings are plentiful in a rustic setting with natural ridges. There are also plenty of wooded areas and trails around the lake to provide a second level of adventure. Most locals my and Angie's age have fond memories of camping and fishing with their families in the 1970s and '80s.

Bluestone Lake is a flood-controlled reservoir on the New River. Be on the lookout for beautiful specimens like bald eagles and otters, but keep in mind snakes live here, too. You can also camp in the area (cabin rentals are available) and go boating on the lake. Nearby Pipestem State Park offers zip-lining, mountain biking, and guided fishing excursions for even more thrills.

In Hinton on WV 3 and 20
recreation.gov/camping/gateways/314

TAILGATE
AT A WVU MOUNTAINEER FOOTBALL GAME

Attending a WVU football game is electrifying, beginning with tailgating in the Blue Lot, which fans take very seriously. Milan Puskar Stadium packs in 60,000 rowdy fans. As soon as you hear the first drumbeat of "The Pride of West Virginia," WVU's marching band, you know, win or lose, it is a good day to be a Mountaineer. The excitement is palpable when the team hits the field and 60,000 fans rise to their feet to cheer.

One way to get the people in the stands and the team fired up is with the "Let's go, Mountaineers" chant, where one side starts, "Let's go," and the other answers back, "Mountaineers." After a win, queue John Denver's "Take Me Home, Country Roads" for the best part of the day.

Milan Puskar Stadium
One Ira Errett Rodgers Dr., Morgantown 26505
(304) 293-5621, wvusports.com/sports/football and bands.wvu.edu/ensembles/mountaineer-marching-band

BATHE IN THE MINERAL WATERS
OF BERKELEY SPRINGS

Berkeley Springs, known as America's first spa, is where Founding Father George Washington chose respite in a warm mineral spa over 250 years ago.

Today, Berkeley Springs still attracts guests to do the same, with multiple options, in the constant 74.3-degree spring waters. This steeped-in-tradition ritual is available to anyone, with services ranging from a soak to a sauna and shower, as well as all the typical spa services like body treatments, aromatherapy, and massage.

Services take place in the historic Roman and main bathhouses. Reservations are preferred, but they do accept walk-ins. For a 20-minute soak in the main bathhouse, guests are led to private quarters to change into a cozy robe and slippers. The historic Old Roman Bathhouse has longer soaking times, though the private chambers are not as plush.

Two S Washington St., Berkeley Springs 25411
(304) 258-2711, wvstateparks.com/park/berkeley-springs-state-park

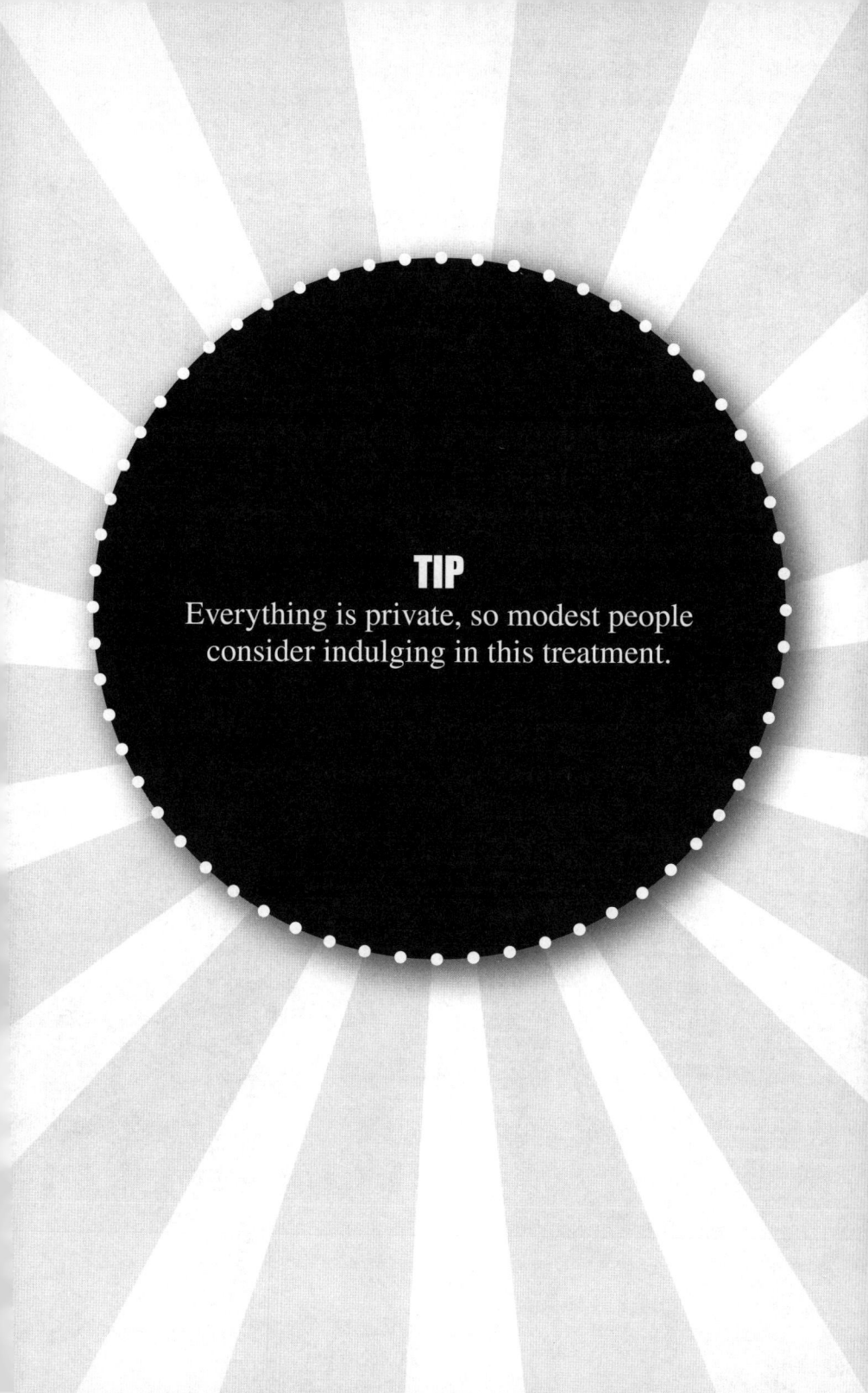

Bavarian Inn

Fiesta dishes at Tamarack

The West Virginia Coal Miner
at the West Virginia State Capitol Complex

The Greenbrier Resort Hotel Hallway

Hovatter's Wildlife Zoo

Mystery Hole

Palace of Gold

Snowshoe Village

Frostop Drive-In root beer floats

Taylor Books

Mothman Statue in Point Pleasant

Watoga Lake

CULTURE AND HISTORY

SIGN UP
FOR A FREE BLENKO GLASS FACTORY TOUR

Blenko Glass Visitor Center in Milton offers a vast collection of hand-blown and cast glassware that is the pride of the Mountain State. The handcrafted glass pieces, namely the iconic 384 Water Bottle, have been sold in the United States since 1893. Other glass items include suncatchers, ornaments, and vases in a rainbow of colors.

Guided tours are free of charge yet require a reservation and include the glass museum (with many one-of-a-kind pieces), a tour of the working facility and skilled artisans, and a condensed explanation of the 100-year-old glass business with a name known worldwide. Closed-toed shoes and eye protection (provided) are required.

Nine Bill Blenko Dr., Milton 25541
(304) 743-9081, blenko.com/pages/visit-blenko

DID YOU KNOW?
You may have seen Blenko glassware at New York's St. Patrick's Cathedral, the White House, DC's National Cathedral, and Colonial Williamsburg. It is also the trophy for the Country Music Awards.

ADMIRE
THE WEST VIRGINIA STATE CAPITOL

I am biased, but if you've seen our state capitol glistening in the sunlight, the gold dome jutting into the sky and reflecting so beautifully on the Kanawha River, you may agree it is the most gorgeous. The West Virginia State Capitol building, designed by architect Cass Gilbert, is open to tour every day of the week. Stunning marble walls and floors decorate the inside, while the capitol rotunda (with a 4,000-pound chandelier) makes a perfect spot for photo ops and special occasions.

The WV State Capitol is just as lovely on the outside, patterned after the US Capitol in Washington, DC. Immaculate gardens, handsome statues, war memorials, and water fountains dot the landscape, while cute squirrels frolic on the lawn. Don't miss the carved heads of mythological creatures above the building's entranceways.

1900 Kanawha Blvd E, Charleston 25305
(304) 558-4839 for tours
wvlegislature.gov/educational/citizens/guide.cfm

DID YOU KNOW?
WV has the highest dome of all state capitals and is five feet taller than the United States Capitol.

West Virginia Capitol Building

OVERNIGHT
AT HOTEL MORGAN

A newer offering to the Morgantown landscape is a juxtaposition of old and new. The Hotel Morgan is a beautiful Wyndham boutique hotel property, "a landmark reborn," that opened in 2020 with 81 luxury hotel rooms (and two suites), a stylish bar and restaurant, plus an eye-catching lobby with a cascade of sparkling chandeliers. Hotel room features that won me over were the retro refrigerators, high-end bathrooms, brass keys, and custom wardrobes. Hotel Morgan occupies the building where the first Hotel Morgan, circa 1922, sat on High Street.

If you can afford the splurge, stay in the Chancellor's Suite (797 square feet), a sensational indulgence that can sleep four, though you may not want to leave. The coffee and craft cocktails from Anvil + Ax are worth trying. If you are hungry, go for the homemade peanut butter, bacon, and caramelized banana panini.

127 High St., Morgantown 26505
(304) 292-8200, hotelmorgan.com

EXPLORE
THE BECKLEY EXHIBITION COAL MINE

You're in coal country when you travel to West Virginia. Perhaps the best place to learn about the coal industry and see the progress of this career trade is at the Beckley Exhibition Coal Mine. The site where Angie and I took field trips as kids to ride deep into the underground mines takes on a more refined look these days as the site is now geared to tourists from around the world.

Not only can you see the nonworking 1889 Phillips-Sprague Mine, but you also experience a re-created coal camp property with historic buildings moved to the address for educational purposes. There are a coal camp store, church, school, coal company, and superintendent houses. The Exhibition Coal Mine is also the site for the Youth Museum, which is cleverly made up of railroad box cars and is great fun for all ages.

513 Ewart Ave., Beckley 25801
(304) 256-1747, beckley.org/coal-mine

AWE
OVER THE PALACE OF GOLD

Near Wheeling, you'll find a unique attraction that many West Virginians still do not know exists. The Prabhupada's Palace of Gold started as a home for Srila Prabhupada to write and live a peaceful life. The simple property was way overbuilt into a massive piece of art and is now a spectacular religious pilgrimage site for those seeking the Hare Krishna religion.

Palace of Gold, with 22 karat gold, is open to the public for daily tours from 9 a.m. to 5 p.m. that will run you around $12 for adults and $6 for children ages 6 to 16. It is rumored George Harrison of the Beatles was one of the most memorable guests back in the 1970s. Be sure to see the award-winning picturesque Rose Garden that houses 3,000 bushes.

3759 McCrearys Ridge Rd., Moundsville 26041
(304) 312-8704, palaceofgold.com

EXAMINE
THE LOCAL WILDLIFE IN UPSHUR COUNTY

Located near Buckhannon is the West Virginia State Wildlife Center; the zoological facility aims to help visitors better understand West Virginia wildlife. As you walk along a paved 1.25-mile trail that loops around large enclosures in a hardwood forest, you will discover many species you would not typically see in the wild.

A large field of mature elk is magnificent to watch as they meander around the property or relax in the shade. You will also find other native animals such as boar, coyote, eagles, a wolf, opossum, fox, and a great horned owl, to name a few. Bring the family, pack a picnic, and enjoy the picnic area while spending the day seeing these gorgeous animals.

163 Wildlife Rd., French Creek 26218
(304) 924-6211, wvdnr.gov/outdoor-recreation/west-virginia-wildlife-center

DID YOU KNOW?
French Creek Freddie is the famous local celebrity weather-predicting star of the West Virginia Wildlife Center's Groundhog Day.

VISIT BRAMWELL'S
MILLIONAIRE MANSIONS

Once home to the most millionaires per capita in the country, the tiny town of Bramwell (eight miles from Bluefield) was where wealthy, elite coal barons made their homes in the early 1900s. It was dubbed "Home of Millionaires." Many of these lavish Victorian and Tudor mansions and homes still have the original woodwork, lead and stained glass windows, and even ballrooms. The quaint town, dressed in brick-lined sidewalks and pretty gardens, adds to the backdrop of these picturesque pockets of living history.

Experience a tour of these well-preserved homes in June of each year during the Bramwell Spring Tour of Homes. A few you might see along the way are the Pack, Thomas, Edward Cooper, Jairus Collins, and Isaac T. Mann houses.

bramwellwv.com/townevents.html

DID YOU KNOW?
The Jairus Collins House has original Louis Comfort Tiffany stained glass windows.

TOUR THE AWESOME
WEST VIRGINIA STATE MUSEUM

The free attraction on the WV State Capitol Complex is the West Virginia State Museum, but locals like myself will always refer to it as the Cultural Center, where we took school field trips back in the day. The WV State Museum has a nice mix of permanent and touring exhibits, including a walk through a coal mine exhibit, a replica of historic downtown Charleston via Scott Brothers Drug Store, and a look at frontier life at the popular log cabin exhibit.

Witness the amazing arsenal of West Virginia–made products in the *Celebrating WV* room and *A Legacy of Craftsmanship*. You won't want to miss the well-appointed gift shop either, stocked full of jewelry, souvenirs, books, gourmet foods, glass, and fine art. The museum is closed Sundays and Mondays.

1900 Kanawha Blvd. E, #435, Charleston 25305
(304) 558-0220, wvculture.org

DID YOU KNOW?
The WV State Museum has recently branched out. It has locations at Grave Creek Archaeological Complex, Camp Washington Carver, and Independence Hall.

EXPERIENCE APPALACHIAN CULTURE
VIA LIVING HISTORY AT HERITAGE FARM

Step back into the days of yore through the living history of costumed interpreters and exhibits at Huntington's Heritage Farm Museum and Village, a re-created 19th-century Appalachian village. Points of interest include seven award-winning museums, artisans, and animal exhibits (plus a petting zoo with llamas, piglets, bunnies, and more). You can also check out the new Adventure Park with a ropes course, zip line, and mountain bike park. My favorite parts are the progress (starting with an 1850's Appalachian home), industry, and country store museums. The blacksmith shop, potter's cabin, and sawmill are also popular, as is the picturesque log church.

Heritage Farm Museum, a Smithsonian Affiliate, is open for visitors Fridays and Saturdays, June through October. It hosts special events, including a Fall Festival and Christmas Village, later in the year.

3300 Harvey Rd., Huntington, 25704
(304) 522-1244, heritagefarmmuseum.com

TIP
Let the little ones burn off steam at the Six Simple Machines Discovery Zone playground.

JAUNT THROUGH
THE MUSEUM OF AMERICAN GLASS

The Museum of American Glass in Weston was created in 1993 to showcase the state's well-known glass industry. It was designed to preserve our state's precious rich glass producer heritage through education and tourism. The museum offers free admission for those wishing to view the collection of local glassware and sparkling cut-glass pieces from around the world—20,000-plus to be exact. The dazzling collection includes Blenko and Fenton, two locally made WV glassware brands that are world famous.

Other points of interest at this stop include the National Marble Museum and the second most extensive display of Steuben art glass. Self-guided tours and a research library with 1,500 publications are available. Allow an hour or so for your tour. Don't miss the Vaseline glass, uranium glass that is usually yellow or greenish in color and glows when a UV light hits it.

230 W Main Ave., Weston 26452
(304) 269-5006, magwv.com

GRAB A SELFIE
WITH DON KNOTTS

Andy Griffith fans will relish the fact that leading funnyman Deputy Sheriff Barney Fife, Don Knotts, was from West Virginia. A life-size statue in his likeness sits on High Street in front of the Metropolitan Theatre in downtown Morgantown. Artist Jamie Lester designed the statue of Knotts seated on a pedestal, holding his Barney Fife hat, in 2016. A star is also on the sidewalk dedicated to the famous actor and comedian. Knotts was raised in Morgantown, got his bachelor's degree from West Virginia University, and returned to visit often. He won five Emmys for his work on *The Andy Griffith Show*.

Knotts developed lung cancer and passed away in 2005 from complications of pneumonia. However, his presence was and is still felt in Morgantown, where he even has a street (Don Knotts Boulevard) named after him.

371 High St., Morgantown 26505

WALK AROUND HARPERS FERRY:
WV'S CIVIL WAR PAST

One of the most important attractions at Harpers Ferry National Historical Park is John Brown's Fort. On September 12–15, 1862, Brown and an abolitionist group forcibly took the federal armory and held hostages, known as the triggering incident of the American Civil War. The event is documented well at the park and the Battle of Harpers Ferry site.

Guests can park at the visitor center parking lot and ride the shuttle bus down to Lower Town or park at one of the spaces at Lower Town, which are extremely limited. Points of interest include the John Brown Museum, Bolivar Heights, Murphy Farm, Meriwether Lewis Museum, a tavern, a dry-goods store, a candy store, and a bookshop. The Harpers Ferry historic site sits at the confluence of the Potomac and Shenandoah Rivers.

171 Shoreline Dr., Harpers Ferry 25425
(304) 535-6029, nps.gov/hafe/index.htm

DID YOU KNOW?
You can walk the picturesque pedestrian bridge to the C&O Canal National Historical Park towpath.

PUSH YOUR FRIGHTS
TO THE LIMITS IN MOUNDSVILLE

West Virginia has a second paranormal site to visit in Moundsville. The West Virginia Penitentiary, circa 1876, is a gothic attraction with turrets and battlements (think a castle) with a history including fires, riots, murders, and dozens of electric chair and hanging executions. Its inmates believe that if you die in prison, your soul remains, so many tortured souls should be roaming the scene.

Guests can choose from an array of public and private tours at the DOJ's "Top Ten Most Violent Correctional Facilities," with even more offerings during Halloween. Regular tours are wheelchair accessible. If you are a fan of escape rooms, you can "escape the pen" with a group of four to eight.

818 Jefferson Ave., Moundsville 26041
(304) 845-6200, wvpentours.com

FUN FACT
This facility, which operated as a prison until 1995, has no air conditioning or heating, so dress accordingly.

STEP BACK IN TIME
AT BLENNERHASSETT ISLAND

I was 53 years old when I finally realized the magnificence of Blennerhassett Island, a historic property in Parkersburg. To reach the island, now a state park, you can take the daily sternwheeler riverboat ferry or go via private vessel. Purchase tickets for the ferry ride to Blennerhassett Island State Park at the Blennerhassett Museum of Regional History on Juliana Street. The *Island Belle* boat ride on the Ohio River from Point Park will get you to the historical property in about 20 minutes.

Once there, you can tour the Palladian mansion, book an island tour via horse-drawn carriage-wagon ride, or wander on foot. If you enjoy bike riding, you can bring your own bike or rent one on the island for under $5 per hour. The horse-drawn wagon ride has a live narrated tour and allows you to see much of the island. Blennerhassett Island is open from May through the end of October.

137 Juliana St., Parkersburg 26101
(304) 420-4800
wvstateparks.com/park/blennerhassett-island-historical-state-park

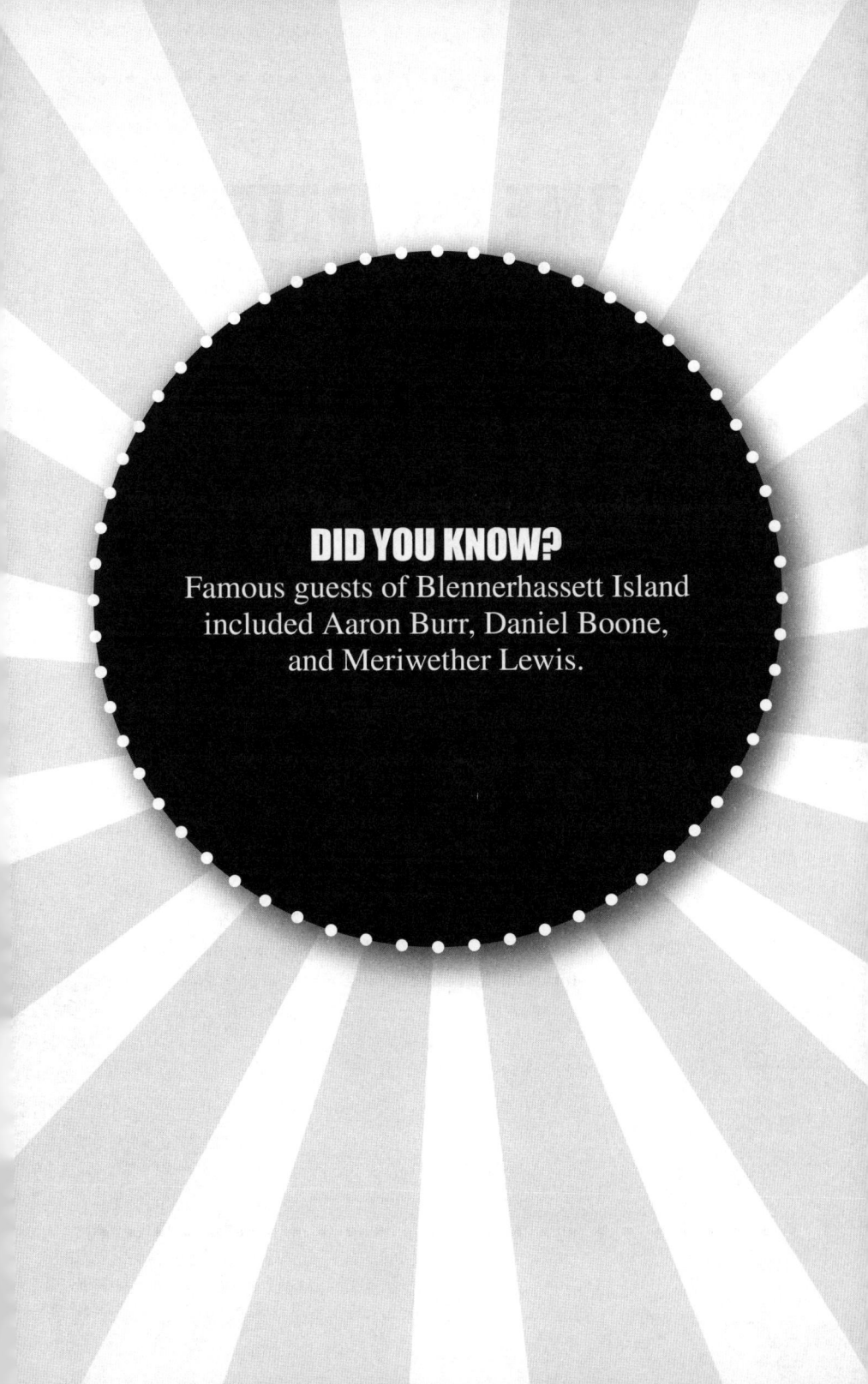

DID YOU KNOW?
Famous guests of Blennerhassett Island included Aaron Burr, Daniel Boone, and Meriwether Lewis.

70

BECOME COMPETENT
IN NATIVE WILDLIFE, FLORA, AND FAUNA

The Claudia L. Workman Wildlife Education Center at Forks of Coal Natural Area in Alum Creek is a newer wildlife education center managed by the WV Division of Natural Resources and worthy of a visit. Here, you can learn about native wildlife, conservation, forestry, and stream restoration. The beautiful center is a labor of love and dedication, apparent in the state-of-the-art exhibits and displays. Visitors can also learn to identify native plants and animals and participate in hosted family-friendly outdoor events. There are also nearly five miles of trails along the paths with Coal River history signage.

One of the latest additions is a pollinator and wildlife viewing field cultivated with grasses and wildflowers. The center is a free attraction and also has free on-site parking.

50 Rocky Branch Rd., Alum Creek 25003
wvdnr.gov/claudia-l-workman-wildlife-education-center-at-forks-of-coal-state-natural-area

WANDER
THE HUNTINGTON MUSEUM OF ART

Art fans will love the Huntington Museum of Art, a nationally accredited museum and also the largest in the state, with 60,000 square feet dedicated to fine art, glassware, a plant conservatory, and a great gift shop. Admission is $5 (and free on Tuesdays). The exhibits are interesting enough to take up a few hours of your time. Besides paintings and portraits, there is an exciting Herman Dean Firearms Gallery, and the Decorative Arts Gallery with much glassware—like 1,000 pieces.

The plant conservatory is top notch. Its collection includes cacao, sugarcane, cashew, coffee plants/trees, and many tropical and subtropical flowers you would not see in this country. And there are over 100 orchids. The focal point of the whole property is *The Huntington Museum of Art Tower*, a 127-by-69-by-62-inch Dale Chihuly glass piece that is absolutely breathtaking. The museum is closed Mondays.

2033 McCoy Rd., Huntington 25701
(304) 529-2701, hmoa.org

PAY TRIBUTE
TO THE FALLEN MINERS

West Virginia was the site of the 2010 Upper Big Branch Mining Disaster in Montcoal that took the lives of 29 workers when an explosion 1,000 feet underground shook and crumbled the earth. Twenty-nine men perished from a huge number of corporate safety violations, but mostly of high levels of methane and coal dust in a space lacking the required ventilation systems. Our community was devastated. These were our friends, family, neighbors, and fellow West Virginians.

A somber 48-foot black granite monument at Upper Big Branch Miners Memorial Plaza pays tribute to our fallen miners in Whitesville, Boone County. It has the miners' silhouettes etched across the front, and interpretive signs sit in a peaceful parklike setting along the Coal River. First responders and those who helped in the face of danger are also listed on the memorial. This is a beautiful place to pay respects to those fallen, and those still going underground today.

38175 Coal River Rd., Whitesville 25209
ubbminersmemorial.com

STOP BY
THE FIRST AFRICAN AMERICAN WORLD WAR I MEMORIAL

Spend some time at a memorial dedicated to African American soldiers. Of the 58,000 West Virginia men who served during World War I, 1,500 African Americans signed up from the Appalachian region of McDowell County. Built by architect Hassell Hicks, the Kimball War Memorial opened in 1928, paying tribute to their service and dedication.

The classical revival stone, brick, and terra cotta building originally included a meeting and trophy room, library, kitchen, and rec center. It was rented out for special occasions; jazz legend Cab Calloway once performed there. The Kimball War Memorial was restored in 2006 and now serves as a cultural resource, programming center, and social hub for the community. Its exhibits share the story of the rural Southern coal miners who served in WWI through exhibits and photographs. The Kimball War Memorial is open for tours Monday through Friday.

78 One Way St., Kimball 24853
(304) 585-7789, easygrants.info/forgotten-legacy-wwi

SHOPPING AND FASHION

LEARN ABOUT
WORLD-FAMOUS FIESTA DINNERWARE

One may be surprised that a top name in everyday dishes, also used around the world, is made here in the Mountain State. Homer Laughlin is the parent company behind the popular and colorful Fiesta tableware line. They have been in business for 150 years! These durable dishes can go from the dishwasher to the microwave and even the oven. You can purchase Fiesta dinnerware as a collection, with several new items coming out annually and some retiring, or for everyday use. Plus, they make your dinner table look lovely.

Want Fiesta but need a bargain? You can buy seconds via the store and tent sales at Everything Fiesta in Sutton and Fiesta Factory in Newell, where the company is based. Famous TV shows and movies where you can see Fiesta tableware include *Modern Family*, *Two and a Half Men*, *The Big Bang Theory*, and *Meet the Fockers*.

Fiesta Factory
672 Fiesta Dr., Newell 26050
(304) 387-1300, fiestafactorydirect.com

Everything Fiesta
52 Skidmore Ln., Sutton 26601
(304) 765-5383

Everything Fiesta in Sutton

75

OBSERVE
THE WORLD-CLASS TAMARACK

Tamarack is a premier shopping and dining destination for handmade West Virginia products from over 2,800 artisans representing all 55 counties. These one-of-a-kind treasures include Fiesta dishes, pottery, handmade furniture, artwork from the most talented painters (including my dad, David Richards), and home decor. You will also find gourmet food items such as jams, jellies, salsas, and candies. Even art classes are offered to give guests a hands-on experience at glassblowing supervised by the resident glassblowing expert.

The chef overseeing the onsite restaurant is from the Greenbrier Resort, so the food is impeccable. Look for the famous Greenbrier peaches to take home and enjoy, or try the peach cobbler at the restaurant.

One Tamarack Park, Beckley 25801
(304) 256-6843, tamarackwv.com

FUN FACT

My mother and grandmother were selected by the juried process and sold homemade dolls at Tamarack in the mid-'90s. They chose my grandmother's Christmas ornament for the White House Christmas tree.

BUY LOCAL
AT ORR'S FARM MARKET

What began as a 60-acre farm in 1954 is now well over 1,000 acres and produces more than just fruits. Orr's Farm Market offers pick-your-own options with blueberries, strawberries, cherries, pumpkins, apples, and even flowers. The expansion of the farm has also brought in a gorgeous farm stand complete with a bakery, locally made gourmet foods, gift items, fresh produce, and so much more. They offer an area where you can purchase tickets to see adorable barnyard animals such as mini-horses, goats, bunnies, and sheep.

Purchasing fresh produce from a family-owned farm allows you to have the freshest produce since it was most likely picked from the vines that day. You also get to know the farmers personally. That makes shopping at Orr's Farm Market extra special. Trust me, you do not want to miss their apple cider slushes and doughnuts at the bakery! Orr's is closed Sundays.

682 Orr Dr., Martinsburg 25403
(304) 263-1168, orrsfarmmarket.com

SNAG SOME GOODIES
AT THE BRIDGE ROAD SHOPS

Shopping enthusiasts will delight in the local boutiques known as the Bridge Road Shops in Charleston. These stores, many thriving in the Kanawha Valley for 20-plus years, offer an alternative to downtown Charleston and mall shopping in a lovely neighborhood setting. Locally owned shops include Eggplant (gifts, stationery, and home decor), Geraniums (ladies' clothing and accessories), Charlie Boutique (trendy fashions), and Yarid's Shoes (high-end shoes, boots, accessories, and purses), to name a few.

The Bridge Road Shops also have restaurants, a fantastic bakery (Sarah's, with impeccable pastries, quiche, and cake balls), yoga and pilates classes, and a jewelry store. Parking is free. The Bridge Road Shops encourage holiday shoppers to visit and buy their gorgeous holiday decor and gifts through a top-notch seasonal Holiday Open House event, typically in mid-November.

1011 Bridge Rd., Charleston 25314
(address for Eggplant: centralized location)
(304) 346-3525, bridgeroad.org

PARTICIPATE
IN A QUILT HOP

The popularity of quilting is at an all-time high. Whether you are a quilter, want to learn quilting, or just enjoy looking at beautiful finished products like I do, you can do that at Country Road Quilt Shop in Morgantown. This 12-year-old business can be found at Seneca Glass Center, a complex with retail shops and the landmark red water tower.

See the website for beginner and advanced quilting classes, shop books, notions, and a fabulous fabric inventory, such as Moda, batik, Riley Blake, and holiday. They are closed on Sundays and participate in local shop hops like WV Hidden Treasures with shops in Buckhannon, Bridgeport, and Reedsville.

709 Beechurst Ave., Ste. 27, Morgantown 26505
(304) 241-5645, countryroadsquilts.com

79

PURCHASE GOURMET FOOD
AND KITCHENWARES IN LEWISBURG

Fancy a shop with lavish gourmet food products, an arsenal of domestic and international wines, high-end kitchen products (think Le Creuset, OXO, and USA Bakeware), and beautiful tableware items? Bella, the Corner Gourmet in historic downtown Lewisburg, checks all the boxes and can help your next get-together stand out.

Before West Virginia experienced the local foods and charcuterie board phenomena, Bella, the Corner Gourmet, had already made its mark and secured its customer base. From mango and triple-cream artisan cheeses to superior jarred olives and pasta sauces, you will discover everything you need and could want in this gem. Don't miss the darling salt and pepper shakers, Catstudio pieces, and fine tea selections.

1017 Washington St. E, Lewisburg 24901
(304) 520-4921, bellagourmetwv.com

DID YOU KNOW?
Bella's creates gorgeous custom gift baskets.

CHECK OUT THE ANTIQUE SHOPPING
IN BERKELEY SPRINGS

Berkeley Springs is a quaint little town perfect for walking around and taking in the local history. A big part of Berkeley Springs' popularity is its antique and unique shops. There are several antique shops around town; you could spend hours and still not see every little treasure from the past. The Berkeley Springs Antique Mall has a vast china and crystal collection, but that is just the beginning of what you will find here. The shop is well stocked, labeled, and organized.

Berkeley Springs Memories is perfect for finding nostalgic candies, mineral water from the local spring, and even fun Christmas and seasonal items. If you are looking for specialty food items, stop by Fleur de Lis Cheese Shop for your charcuterie needs. This little town is full of treasures for everyone.

Berkeley Springs Antique Mall
Seven Fairfax St., Berkeley Springs 25411
(304) 258-5676, berkeleysprings.com/shop/berkeley-springs-antique-mall

Berkeley Springs Memories
15 N Washington St., Berkeley Springs 25411
(304) 258-2000, facebook.com/BerkeleySpringsMemories

Fleur de Lis Cheese Shop
15 Fairfax Rd., Berkeley Springs 25411
(727) 742-8333, fleurdelischeeseshop.com

SHOP LOCALLY
AT GRITT'S FARM

The experience of visiting Gritt's Farm has evolved into so much more than just shopping for freshly picked produce and seasonal flowers to decorate your home and garden. It has become a fun family destination. You may find yourself sliding down the slide mountain, playing in the corn bin, or riding around the farm on a tractor-pulled hayride.

Spring and summer seasons, you will find the healthiest flowers to either transplant to your own flower bed or potted plants that need no further effort other than choosing the perfect spot. In the fall, they have a corn maze, pumpkin patch, games, and lots of yummy treats that keep guests returning yearly. If you cannot make the trip to Buffalo to the farm, you can also purchase fresh produce and flowers at their site at Capitol Market in Charleston.

864 Gritt Rd., Buffalo 25033
(304) 937-2565, grittsfarm.com

FANGIRL
AT BARNWOOD LIVING

A popular Magnolia Network TV show is filmed around the country, with its home base or "boneyard" in West Virginia. You will find a retail shop, Barnwood Living, dedicated to the Barnwood Boho lifestyle in White Sulphur Springs, with a mix of home goods, gifts, men's and women's clothing, and gear worn by the show's crew.

If you have a fan of the show in your family, you will want to visit the shop for a souvenir T-shirt, hat, or even a leather tool belt. The shop's ambience and vibe reflect the show's passion for restoring the past with a touch of modern flair. The slogan "Work Hard, Be Kind, Take Pride" is a phrase by which Mark Bowe and his crew live. It shines through in the shows and retail location.

574 Main St. W, White Sulphur Springs 24986
(888) 941-9553, shopbarnwoodliving.com

HANG OUT
AT THE BELOVED TAYLOR BOOKS

Since opening its doors in 1995 in the heart of downtown Charleston, Taylor Books has become one of the most iconic shops in the capital city. One of the most famous repeat visitors is WV's own Jennifer Garner, who has been spotted many times during her trips home to visit family. For folks who work in the downtown Charleston area, the shop's café is a daily stop for morning coffee and made-fresh daily pastries. Other menu items include fresh salads, soup, quiche, fruit, and upscale desserts.

Taylor Books has a wide variety of new and used books, magazines, cards, and gifts. They also have wonderful selections of children's and West Virginia–related books. You will want to allow yourself plenty of time to browse this fabulous bookshop. Have a seat, relax, and enjoy your purchase with a delicious latte and scone.

226 Capitol St., Charleston 25301
(304) 342-1461, taylorbooks.com

IMMERSE YOURSELF
IN HELVETIA'S INTERNATIONAL FLAVOR

Helvetia, on the National Register of Historic Places since 1978, is a small town tucked deep into the high mountains of Randolph County. Swiss and German immigrants from Brooklyn formed the town after the Civil War. Once word spread across the US and Canada, the new settlement grew from six to 308. Since many of the original descendants still live in the area, you'll find that many of the traditions from their home countries are still true today.

The annual Helvetia Community Fair is the perfect time to visit, with artisans selling crafts and homemade food items. The community parade, with creative floats showcasing the Swiss and German heritage, is one of the day's many highlights. Plan to eat dinner at the Hütte Restaurant, offering a sampling of delicious Swiss and German meals. Be sure to stop by the general store for locally made cheese.

4916 Pickens Rd., Helvetia 26224
(304) 924-9100, swissrootswv.com

85

STROLL THROUGH
HISTORIC DOWNTOWN SHEPHERDSTOWN

The main street through Shepherdstown (German Street) has an eclectic mix of shopping and dining opportunities. Since the town is the home of Shepherd University, you will encounter a youthful feel in some of the shops while holding true to the area's historical value.

One of the oldest shops is O'Hurley's General Store, where you can find almost everything imaginable, from antique toys to horse supplies.

As you wander the streets, you will discover a wide variety of locally owned boutiques offering a fantastic selection of clothing, wine, books, and art in several galleries. If dining is what you are looking for, look no further; Shepherdstown has you covered. There are coffee shops, an Irish pub, a diner, a bakery, and Asian fusion cuisine, just to name a few. Be sure to stop and visit this quaint little mountain town.

CHECK OUT SOME SHEPHERDSTOWN SHOPS

Mountaineer Popcorn Company
102 E German St., Shepherdstown 25443
(410) 937-4612, mountaineerpopcorn.com

Shepherdstown Sweet Shop
100 W German St., Shepherdstown 25443
(304) 876-2432, wvbakery.com

O'Hurley's General Store
205 E Washington St., Shepherdstown 25443
(304) 876-6907, ohurleys.com

Four Seasons Books
116 W German St., Shepherdstown 25443
(304) 876-3486, fourseasonsbooks.com

Famous Room at The Greenbrier Resort

UNIQUELY WEST VIRGINIA

EXPAND YOUR PALATE WITH A WV TRADITION:
RAMPS

Chow down at Feast of the Ramson in the ramp capital of the world: Richwood, West Virginia. This highly anticipated event, 80-plus years strong, takes place in May. The feast with indoor and outdoor seating includes an Appalachian meal with brown beans, corn bread, potatoes, ham, and of course, ramps, with desserts and cold drinks. Local musicians add festive music, and you can also enjoy an arts-and-crafts show.

In a nutshell, a ramp is a pungent onion and wild plant that grows in the mountains of Appalachia. Once you smell a ramp, you won't soon forget it and may still be smelling it days later. Ramps are close relatives to onions and garlic and are sometimes called wild leeks. Ramps fried in bacon grease in scrambled eggs are my favorite way to enjoy them. You'll find roadside ramp stands selling ramps from March to May.

20 Ave. B, Richwood 26261
(304) 846-6790, richwoodchamberofcommerce.org/feast-of-the-ramson

NAVIGATE
TO THE HIGHEST POINT IN WEST VIRGINIA

Going to the highest point in each state should be a bucket list item. If you've ever driven to one, you know the excitement and thrill of the steep roads, change of wind and weather, and sheer beauty when you reach the top. Spruce Knob is West Virginia's highest point, and the drive to get there is half the fun. Expect to snake up a steep, curvy road, probably twenty minutes before you reach the acme. There are no guardrails, so be prepared for a thrilling drive, but there are pull-over points along the way for taking photos.

At the top, you'll have a short hike to get out to the most stellar landing and lookout point. The views are breathtaking, to say the least, and the flora and fauna are sensational.

Spruce Knob Trail, Riverton 26814

TIP
Expect a significant temperature change at the 4,863-foot elevation.

VACATION
AT THE GREENBRIER RESORT

One of the fascinating places in the Mountain State needs little or no introduction. The Greenbrier Resort is "America's Resort," where you can expect world-class luxury. Enjoy a long list of amenities (over 55) and championship golf courses (resort, private, and nine-hole par-3 walking course) as you indulge in the landmark property that has hosted many US presidents and other famous names throughout its history.

Accommodations range from signature resort rooms to legacy cottages and Greenbrier estate homes. A daily ritual at the Greenbrier is afternoon tea service, free to guests, with live music and white-glove service. The 1778 property also boasts high-end retail shops, a fantastic spa, a world-class casino, and even a bunker tour. My favorite offering at the Greenbrier Resort has always been the year-round Christmas Shop at the Depot across the street from the impeccably decorated and luxurious hotel.

101 W Main St., White Sulphur Springs 24986
(855) 453-4858, greenbrier.com

TIP

Other fantastic Greenbrier Resort amenities include aerial adventure course, alpine climbing tower, arcade, bowling, bunker tours, bike rentals, carriage rides, croquet, escape room, e-bikes, falconry, fishing, fitness classes, geocaching, Greenbrier scavenger hunt, gun club, horseback riding, indoor and outdoor pools, Jeep driving adventure, kayaking, paintball challenge, pickleball, Polaris RZR driving adventure, Polaris Slingshot driving adventure, Segway tours, shuffleboard, sleigh rides, stand-up paddleboarding, tennis (indoor and outdoor), and various workshops.

MEET
THE DOLLY SODS WILDERNESS AREA

Dolly Sods Wilderness Area is over 17,000 acres that span three counties—Grant, Randolph, and Tucker—with elevation levels ranging from 2,500 to 4,700 feet. There are 47 miles of hiking trails and an easy one that will take you to the breathtaking views of Bear Rocks, one of the most photographed spots at Dolly Sods.

Whether you are lucky enough to visit on a clear day or even when it's foggy, the scenery is fantastic. You may notice right away that the pine trees at Dolly Sods have limbs on only one side. This is a by-product of the wind blowing from one direction, so over time, the trees have adapted to this environment. Dolly Sods is an easy drive from either Canaan Valley or Petersburg, so make sure you take the time to visit.

Forest Rd. 75, Davis 26260
fs.usda.gov/recarea/mnf/recarea/?recid=12366

Dolly Sods

TRY THE WORLD-FAMOUS
MOUNTAIN STATE FINISHING SALT

The history of salt-making in the Kanawha Valley dates back to the early 1800s. The Dickinson family first drilled for brine in 1817. By the 1850s, hundreds of wells along the Kanawha River could produce millions of salt bushels per year, becoming the largest salt-producing region in the United States.

J. Q. Dickinson Salt-Works brine is derived from the Iapetus Ocean, producing the finest quality of finishing salt, free of metals or contaminants. The 1851 London World's Fair awarded "The Great Kanawha Salt" with the "Best Salt in the World" award. Today, the seventh generation of the Dickinson family has revived the salt-making process. You can tour the salt works in Malden for free, Monday through Saturday, starting on the hour and half hour. There is also an Appalachian Mercantile to taste and purchase the flavored salts and products made with them.

4797 Midland Dr., Malden 25306
(304) 925-7918, jqdsalt.com

ROAD-TRIP KANAWHA FALLS
AND SCENIC ROUTE 60

Taking a road trip through the state is a great way to see the wondrous landscape of our beautiful Mountain State. My favorite is a small portion of Route 60, the Midland Trail Scenic Byway, West Virginia's oldest, from Charleston to Fayetteville. Along this mostly two-lane road, starting in Charleston, you'll pass the Burger Carte in Smithers, where you should stop for ice cream. A little further up is Cathedral Falls, with super-high cascades over a sandstone cliff.

Kanawha Falls spans the width of the Kanawha River, with water pouring over; then, a few feet away is the nearly 200-year-old Glen Ferris Inn, perfect for a home-cooked meal. Continuing on is Chimney Corner Country Store, with Appalachian souvenirs and trinkets. Up next is Hawk's Nest State Park with an amazing overlook. You'll get an eyeful of the majestic New River Gorge National River and can take a tram ride to the bottom for a fun adventure.

PRACTICE YOUR PHOTOGRAPHY
AT BABCOCK STATE PARK

A picture of the iconic Glade Creek Grist Mill from Babcock State Park is one you've most likely seen in major publications and anything having to do with West Virginia. It certainly is beautiful and one of the most photographed spots in the state, jutting atop a boulder-strewn rippling stream. You can see the majestic site up close and personal in Clifftop, minutes from the New River Gorge National River in Fayette County. Come often to capture the sublime attraction in its seasonal landscape setting.

Babcock State Park has 4,127 wooded acres to get lost in or enjoy the rustic landscape. Other points of interest are the primo trout-fishing on Glade Creek and Boley Lake, campgrounds, cabins, and a park headquarters gift shop.

486 Babcock Rd., Clifftop 25831
(304) 438-3004, wvstateparks.com/glade-creek-grist-mill-babcock

---

DID YOU KNOW?
The Glade Creek Grist Mill is a re-creation of the original 1890 Cooper's Mill.

PAY HOMAGE
TO THE FIRST MOTHER'S DAY SITE

The first Mother's Day celebration was held in Grafton. Andrews Methodist Episcopal Church, where founder Anna Jarvis had the idea to celebrate mothers around the country, became the mother church of the Mother's Day celebration in 1908. I, for one, appreciate that she had the insight to pay thanks for the best job one could ever have. Anna's vision was "making the lives of our mothers happier and brighter, and to see where we can improve on the past."

Today, an International Mother's Day Shrine, charted in 1962, is in downtown Grafton, with a park, monument, and several photo ops. It is also a National Historic Landmark of Taylor County. You can see and tour the Anna Jarvis Birthplace Museum four miles south of town on US Route 119/250.

11 East Main St., Grafton 26354
(304) 265-1589 (church)

284 Pearl Felton Ln., Grafton 26354
(304) 265-5549 (museum), internationalmothersdayshrine.org

DID YOU KNOW?
The Anna Jarvis Birthplace Museum was also the first field headquarters of General George McClellan during the Civil War.

SNACK ON
THE ICONIC PEPPERONI ROLL

The most iconic dish associated with West Virginia is the pepperoni roll. This handheld, easy-to-eat, inexpensive snack food will hook you at the first bite. Pepperoni rolls were created as a lunch food for coal miners in the early 20th century. Semisoft white yeast-leavened bread-roll dough is wrapped around a mound of zesty sliced or stick pepperoni and baked to a golden brown. During the baking process, the bread becomes infused with pepperoni oil. The creator of the beloved pepperoni roll, Country Club Bakery in Fairmont (1927), does not use cheese, but several of the newer bakeries do. I like them both ways. Some even come with peppers. Pepperoni rolls need no refrigeration; you can eat them at room temperature or warmed.

1211 Country Club Rd., Fairmont 26554
(304) 363-5690, countryclubbakery.net

DID YOU KNOW?
Country Club Bakery pepperoni rolls are shipped to fans in all 50 states.

Pepperoni Rolls

GAIN AN UNDERSTANDING
OF THE MOTHMAN FOLKLORE

The Mothman of Point Pleasant is West Virginia's most intriguing folklore and what is referred to as "dark tourism." The Mothman, a flying humanoid creature or cryptid, was claimed to be seen in Point Pleasant from November 1966 to December 1967. Events that followed and during the sightings include the collapsed Silver Bridge and many other unexplained phenomena. People come from all over the country, maybe the world, to explore the legend and see the 12-foot metallic silver Mothman statue in Gunn Park, created by Bob Roach. A festival is held in the Mothman's honor every third weekend in September.

You can learn more about the mysterious glowing red-eyed creature at the Mothman Museum. It houses rare historical documents from eyewitnesses and a shop with a huge collection of Mothman souvenirs. You will also see memorabilia from the 2002 supernatural movie *The Mothman Prophecies* starring Laura Linney and Richard Gere.

400 Main St., Point Pleasant 25550
(304) 812-5211, mothmanmuseum.com

96

GLIMPSE ONE OF THE WORLD'S LARGEST THINGS
IN GREEN BANK

It's hard to narrow down the most fascinating things about wild, wonderful West Virginia, but the Green Bank Observatory (GBO) would be high on the list. The town, which they say is the epicenter of the NRQZ ("What is national radio quiet zone, Alex?"), is surrounded by the Monongahela National Forest. It houses a big dog in astronomical research. Originally the National Radio Astronomy Observatory, the first in the nation, circa 1957, it is now the Green Bank Observatory. In layman's terms, it is the most powerful and largest steerable radio telescope in the world. The Robert C. Byrd Green Bank Telescope can clearly make out 85 percent of the things in the sky—think stars, planets, asteroids, etc.—aiding science and astronomy.

The Green Bank Science Center, with hands-on exhibits, will occupy and keep the interest of visiting children.

155 Observatory Rd., Green Bank 24944
(304) 456-2150, greenbankobservatory.org

DID YOU KNOW?
The telescope weighs 17 million pounds.

HIKE TO THE FABULOUS
BLACKWATER FALLS WATERFALL

Blackwater Falls is aptly named for the amber-colored waters cascading over the 62-foot waterfall summit in Tucker County. It is a WV state park and one of the most recognized sites in the Mountain State. Whether you enjoy nature, hiking the 20 miles of trails, or using the viewing platforms for photo ops and the sheer beauty, it is a majestic site. I appreciate the fresh mountain air and variety of red spruce, hemlock, birch, and maple trees equally.

If you can, hike down to the basin of the falls for the best views possible—you can even feel the water splashing you. There are a few other smaller falls at the park, while amenities include a nature center, camping, cross-country skiing, and mountain biking.

1584 Blackwater Lodge Rd., Davis 26260
(304) 259-5216, wvstateparks.com/park/blackwater-falls-state-park

---

TIP
If you visit in winter, you may glimpse the falls iced over.

Blackwater Falls

PHOTOGRAPH THE SMALLEST CHURCH
IN THE LOWER 48

Near the town of Eglon lies what claims to be the smallest church in the lower 48 states, built in 1958, before Hawaii and Alaska entered statehood. Our Lady of the Pines is an adorable tiny Roman Catholic Church with a beautiful setting. Its dimensions run 24 by 12 feet, and the inside holds a few church pews, enough to seat 12. Embroidered lace cloth covers the altar, and the windows have pretty stained glass windows. The stone church with a stately white steeple is in immaculate condition and is a sweet stop for guests to take photos and stretch their legs.

I first encountered this little gem on a drive through the backroads of West Virginia after hiking Blackwater Falls State Park. The physical address says 101 Breedlove Road, but it is right off Route 219. Be sure to sign the guest book in the alcove on the left.

Rte. 219, Horse Shoe Run 26287
(304) 735-3801

99

DRIVE THROUGH
A COVERED BRIDGE

In the town of Philippi, Barbour County, you can experience the site of the first land battle (referred to as "Philippi Races") of the American Civil War. The infantry marched down the hill and across the historic bridge, but little fighting occurred. There were luckily no casualties. That covered yellow poplar bridge was designed by Lemuel Chenoweth and is 285 feet long and 26 feet wide.

The Philippi Covered Bridge on the Tygart Valley River is the only remaining covered bridge on a federal highway, and you can drive through it. It has withstood fires, floods, and ice jams yet remains a favorite photographed landmark. There is also a nice parking spot to get pictures of the bridge from below. I was excited to drive through the covered bridge, as many I've visited around the country are pedestrian-only.

US 250 at the junction with US 119

INVESTIGATE
THE WV BIGFOOT MUSEUM

Just when you thought it was safe to wander the wilderness, come to the West Virginia Bigfoot Museum. For those unfamiliar, the definition of a bigfoot is a large, hairy, apelike creature that resembles a yeti. They are supposedly found in Northwest America. A second definition, "a well-known journalist," makes me want to start putting that term in my bio.

All jokes aside, this one-of-a-kind museum is housed in the Mountain Laurel Country Store in downtown Sutton. It highlights Bigfoot sightings around the Mountain State, including eyewitness accounts, footprint castings (dozens of original casts and cast copies from around the country), and maps of where the sightings occurred. Visit the fun and engaging small-but-mighty museum Wednesday through Saturday.

400 Fourth St., Sutton 2660
(717) 228-7524, facebook.com/WVBigfootMuseum

TIP
While there, check out the country store full of West Virginian artisan crafts and consigners.

Taylor Books

SUGGESTED ITINERARIES

HISTORY LOVERS

Experience Appalachian Culture via Living History at Heritage Farm, 113
Admire the West Virginia State Capitol, 102
Tour the Awesome West Virginia State Museum, 112
Explore the Beckley Exhibition Coal Mine, 105
Step Back in Time at Blennerhassett Island, 118
Pay Homage to the First Mother's Day Site, 153
Walk around Harpers Ferry: WV's Civil War Past, 116

ART & CULTURE LOVERS

Sign Up for a Free Blenko Glass Factory Tour, 100
Wander the Huntington Museum of Art, 121
Gain an Understanding of the Mothman Folklore, 156
Hang Out at the Beloved Taylor Books, 138
Try the World-Famous Mountain State Finishing Salt, 150
Learn about World-Famous Fiesta Dinnerware, 126
Fangirl at Barnwood Living, 137

THRILL SEEKERS

Road-Trip Kanawha Falls and Scenic Route 60, 151
Push Your Frights to the Limits in Moundsville, 117
Find Your Inner Thrill Seeker at ACE Adventure Resort, 75
Pedal a Recycled Railway Line, 73
Plunge West Virginia's Impressive Whitewater Rapids, 56
Ride the Hatfield-McCoy Trail System, 70

FOODIES

Taste the Best Brunch Chicken and Waffles, 7
Get the Scoop on the Best WV Ice Cream Shop, 10
Snack on the Iconic Pepperoni Roll, 154
Feed Your Appetite with Amazing Barbecue at Dem 2 Brothers, 12
Feast at Thyme Bistro, 18
Sample Smooth Ambler Spirits, 14
Stay in a European-Reminiscent Inn, 27

BRING YOUR WHOLE FAMILY ALONG

Dine at a Nostalgic Carhop Eatery, 16
Observe the World-Class Tamarack, 128
Smell the Roses at Ritter Park, 64
Experience Appalachian Culture via Living History at Heritage Farm, 113
Take a Scenic Train Ride in Elkins, 57
Grab a Selfie with Don Knotts, 115
Cozy into a Cabin at the Ashland Resort, 55

• •

Blenko Glassware

Forks of Coal Wildlife

ACTIVITIES
BY SEASON

SPRING

Plunge West Virginia's Impressive Whitewater Rapids, 56
Take a Scenic Train Ride in Elkins, 57
Practice Your Photography at Babcock State Park, 152
Navigate to the Highest Point in West Virginia, 145
Witness WV's Only National Park, 52
Visit Bramwell's Millionaire Mansions, 110

SUMMER

Float on Down the River in St. Albans, 69
Awe over the Palace of Gold, 106
Sleep Outdoors at Watoga, 65
Secure Your Ticket to the West Virginia State Fair, 30
Meet the Dolly Sods Wilderness Area, 148
Splash around Summersville Lake, 72

FALL

Ride the Hatfield-McCoy Trail System, 70

Reminisce at Camden Park, 40

Go Stargazing in Hillsboro, 60

Encounter the Unimaginable at TALA, 33

Chant "We Are Marshall" at a Home Game, 62

WINTER

Hit the Slopes at Snowshoe, 66

Bathe in the Mineral Waters of Berkeley Springs, 78

Celebrate the Holiday Spirit at Oglebay Resort, 68

Sit Courtside at a WVU Basketball Game, 54

Vacation at the Greenbrier Resort, 146

Journey through Organ Cave, 44

INDEX

Abolitionist Ale Works, 24
ACE Adventure Resort, 75, 166
Adelphia Sports Bar & Grille, 63
Adventures on the Gorge, 56
Almost Heaven Desserts & Coffee Shop, 21
Alum Creek, 120
Andrews Methodist Episcopal Church, 153
Anna Jarvis Birthplace Museum, 153
Ansted, 41
Anvil + Ax, 104
Ashland Resort, 55, 166
Avampato Discovery Museum, 38
Babcock State Park, 152, 169
Barnwood Living, 137, 165
Basil's Sports Bar & Grill, 63
Battle Run Campground, 72
Batton Hollow Winery, 6
Bavarian Brothers Brewing, 27
Bavarian Inn, 27, 81
Beaver Creek, 65
Beckley, 9, 17, 105, 128, 165
Beckley Exhibition Coal Mine, 105, 165
Bella, the Corner Gourmet, 133
Ben-Ellen Donuts, 30
Benwood, 9
Berkeley Springs, 24, 78, 134, 135, 170
Berkeley Springs Antique Mall, 80, 134–135
Berkeley Springs Brewing Co., 24

Berkeley Springs Memories, 134–135
Big Timber Brewing Co., 24
Bissonnette Garden, 68
Blackwater Falls State Park, 61, 160
Black Sheep Burrito and Brews, 7
Blenko Glass Co., 100–101, 165, 167
Blenko Glass Visitor Center, 100
Blennerhassett Island State Park, 118–119, 165
Blennerhassett Museum of Regional History, 118
Bluefield, 17, 110
Bluestone Lake, 76
Boley Lake, 152
Bolivar Heights, 116
Bramwell, 110, 169
Bramwell Spring Tour of Homes, 110
Bridge Brew Works, 25
Bridge Road Shops, 131
Bridgeport, 9, 21, 51, 132
Bruceton Mills, 24, 53
Buffalo Mountain, 71
Burger Carte, 17, 151
C&O Canal National Historical Park, 116
Cabwaylingo State Forest, 71
Calvin Price State Forest, 60
Camden Park, 28, 40, 170
Camp Washington Carver, 112
Canaan Valley, 148
Canyon Rim Visitor Center, 52

Caperton Planetarium & Theater, 38
Capitol Market, 136
Capitol Street, 10, 20
Carnegie Hall, 22
Carnegie Hall Gallery, 22
Cass Scenic Railroad, 57
Cathedral Falls, 151
Ceredo, 9
Charles Town, 24, 46
Charleston, 2–4, 7, 9–10, 12, 20–21, 23–24, 32, 38, 43, 63, 69, 102, 112, 131, 136, 138, 151
Charlie Boutique, 131
Cheat River Water Trail, 69
Chimney Corner Country Store, 151
Chirico's Ristorante, 9
Chop House, 3
Christmas Shop at the Depot, 146
Christmas Shoppe & More, 31
Chum's Hotdogs, 4
Civil War Discovery Trail, 60
Clarksburg, 19
Claudia L. Workman Wildlife Education Center, 120
Clay Center, 38–39, 97
Clifftop, 152
Cobb Golf Course, 51
Colombo's Restaurant, 9
Coopers Rock State Forest, 53
Country Club Bakery, 154
Country Road Quilt Shop, 132
Cranny Crow Overlook, 61
Culture Center Theater, 43
Custard Stand, 5
Dave's Famous T&L Hot Dogs, 5
Davis, 24, 61, 148, 158
Dem 2 Brothers & a Grill, 12–13, 166
Der Dog Haus, 5

Dolly Sods Wilderness Area, 83, 148, 169
Don Knotts Statue, 115, 166
Droop Mountain Battlefield State Park, 60
Dunbar, 34–35
Dunbar Bingo Hall, 34
Dunmore, 61
Durbin & Greenbrier Valley Railroad, 57
Eggplant, 131
Elkins, 24, 57, 166, 169
Ellen's Homemade Ice Cream, 10
Everything Fiesta, 126
Fairmont, 5, 9, 154
Fayetteville, 11, 23, 25, 52, 151
Feast of the Ramson, 144
Festival of Lights at Oglebay, 68
Fiesta Dinnerware, 82, 126, 128, 165
Fiesta Factory, 126
Fleur de Lis Cheese Shop, 134–135
Forks of Coal State Natural Area, 120
Four Seasons Books, 141
French Creek, 108–109
Frostop Drive-In, 16, 92
Gauley River, 56
Geraniums, 131
Ghent, 23
Glade Creek Grist Mill, ii, 152
Glade Springs Resort Golf Course, 51
Glen Ferris Inn, 151
Good Zoo, 68
Grafton, 153
Grave Creek Archaeological Complex, 112
Green Bank, 157
Green Bank Observatory, 157
Green Bank Science Center, 157

Greenbrier Course at The Greenbrier, 50
Greenbrier Resort, 85, 128, 146–147, 170
Greenbrier River Trail, 73
Greenbrier Valley Brewing, 25
Gritt's Farm, 136
Gunn Park, 156
Haddad Riverfront Park, 32
Harpers Ferry, 116, 165
Harpers Ferry National Historical Park, 116
Harpers Ferry Park Association Bookshop, 116
Hatfield-McCoy Trail System, 55, 70–71, 166, 170
Hawk's Nest State Park, 151
Helvetia, 139
Helvetia Community Fair, 139
Heritage Farm Museum & Village, 113
High Falls of Cheat, 57
High Ground Brewing, 25
Hillbilly Hot Dogs, 5
Hillsboro, 60, 170
Hinton, 76
Historic Downtown Shepherdstown, 140
Holl's Chocolates, 14
Hollywood Casino at Charles Town Races, 46
Horse Shoe Run, 160
Hotel Morgan, 98, 104
Hovatter's Wildlife Zoo, 42, 86
Huntington, 5, 7, 8, 16, 40, 62, 64, 113, 121, 165
Huntington Museum of Art, 121, 165
Hütte Restaurant, 139
Independence Hall, 112
International Mother's Day Shrine, 153
Island Belle Sternwheeler, 118
Jairus Collins House, 110–111

Jim's Steak and Spaghetti House, 8, 87
Joan C. Edward's Stadium, 62
John Brown's Fort, 116
JP Henry's, 63
J.Q. Dickinson Salt Works, 150
Juliet Art Museum, 38
Kanawha Falls, 151, 166
Kanawha River, 32, 102, 150–151
Kegler's Sports Bar & Grille, 63
Kimball, 123
Kimball War Memorial, 123
King Tut Drive-In, 17
Kingwood, 42
Lansing, 56
Leonoro's Spaghetti House, 9
Lesage, 5
Lewisburg, 17, 22, 30, 133
Live on the Levee, 32
Logan, 9, 17, 21, 70–71
Lost Creek, 6
Lost River State Park, 61
Lynn's Drive Inn, 17
Maier Foundation Performance Hall, 38
Malden, 150
Man, 70
Marlinton, 60, 65, 73
Marshall University, 62–63, 88
Marshall University Thundering Herd Football, 62
Martinsburg, 130
Matewan, 71
Mathias, 61
Maxwelton, 14, 25
Meadows at The Greenbrier, 50
Meriwether Lewis Museum, 116
Metropolitan Theatre, 115
Midland Trail Scenic Byway, 151
Milan Puskar Stadium, 77

Milton, 100
Monongahela National Forest, 54, 157
Morgantown, 23, 25, 53–54, 63, 77, 104, 115, 132
Morrison's Drive Inn, 17
Mothman Museum, 156
Mothman Statue, 94, 156, 165
Moundsville, 21, 106, 117, 166
Mountain Laurel Country Store, 162
Mountain Stage, 43
Mountain State Brewing Co., 25
Mountaineer Popcorn Company, 141
Muriale's Italian Kitchen, 9
Murphy Farm, 116
Museum of American Glass, 114
Mystery Hole, 41, 89
National Marble Museum, 114
Newell, 126
New River, 41, 52, 56, 76, 151–152
New River Gorge Bridge, 41, 52
New River Gorge National Park and Preserve, 52
New River Gorge National River, 151–152
Northfork, 55
Nu-Era Bakery, 21
Oak Hill, 75
Oglebay Park
Oglebay Resort, 68, 170
O'Hurley's General Store, 140–141
Old Roman Bath House, 78
Old White Golf Course at The Greenbrier, 50
Oliverio's Ristorante, 9
Organ Cave, 44, 170
Orr's Farm Market, 124, 130
Our Lady of the Pines, 160
Palace of Gold, 90, 106
Parkersburg, 5, 9, 25, 63, 118

Parkersburg Brewing Co., 25
Pasquale's, 9
Peanut Shoppe, 20
Pete Dye Golf Club, 51
Philippi, 161
Philippi Covered Bridge, 161
Pies & Pints, 23
Pipestem State Park, 76
Point Pleasant, 94, 156
Pomona Salt Cave and Spa, 45
Press Room, 26
Princeton, 25
Purple Fiddle, 31
Quality Bake Shoppe, 21
Raven Golf Course, 66
Resort at Glade Springs, 51
Richwood, 144
Ritter Park Rose Garden, 64
Riverton, 145
Robert C. Byrd Green Bank Telescope, 157
Rocco's Ristorante, 9
Ronceverte, 44
Sarah's Bakery, 131
Scenic Route 60, 151, 166
Schoenbaum Stage, 32
Screech Owl Brewing, 24
Secret Sandwich Society, 11
Seneca Glass Center, 132
Seneca Rocks, 58
Seneca State Forest, 61
Shepherd University, 140
Shepherdstown, 26–27, 140–141
Shepherdstown Sweet Shop, 141
Shinnston, 5
Smithers, 17, 151
Smooth Ambler Spirits, 14–15, 166
Snowshoe, 66, 73, 91, 170

Snowshoe Mountain Resort, 66, 67, 73, 91, 170
Sophisticated Hound Brewing, 25
Split Rock Pools, 66
Spring Hill Pastry Shop, 21
Spruce Knob, 145
State Fair of West Virginia, 30, 169
Sterling Drive-In, 17
Sternwheel Regatta, 32
Stewarts Original Hot Dogs, 5
Stillwaters Restaurant, 74
Stonewall Jackson Lake, 74
Stonewall Resort, 74
Stumptown Ales, 24
Summersville, 72, 169
Summersville Lake, 72, 169
Sutton, 5, 162
Tamarack Marketplace, 128–129, 166
Taste of Our Town, 22
Taylor Books, 93, 138, 164–165
Terra Alta, 25
Theatre West Virginia, 36
Thomas, 25, 31
Thyme Bistro, 18, 165
TJ's Sports Garden Restaurant, 63
Tour de Coal, 69
Trans-Allegheny Lunatic Asylum, 33
Tudor's Biscuit World, 2
Twisted Gun Golf Course, 51
Tygart Valley River, 161
Undo's Family Restaurant, 9

Upper Big Branch Miner's Memorial, 122
Watoga State Park, 60, 65
Weathered Ground Brewery, 23
Weirton, 63
Welch, 17
Weston, 18, 33, 114
West Virginia Bigfoot Museum, 162
West Virginia Civil War Trail, 44
West Virginia Mountaineer Basketball, 54, 170
West Virginia Mountaineer Football, 77
West Virginia State Capitol, 84, 102, 112, 165
West Virginia State Museum, 43, 96, 112, 165
West Virginia Penitentiary, 117
West Virginia State Wildlife Center, 108
West Virginia Symphony, 32, 38
West Virginia University, 54, 77, 115, 170
West Virginia University Coliseum, 54
Wharncliffe, 51
Wheeling, 63, 68, 106
White Sulphur Springs, 50, 137, 146
Whitesville, 122
Wonder Bar Steakhouse, 19
Woody's Grill, 75
Yann's Hot Dog Stand, 5
Yarid's Shoes, 131
Youth Museum of Southern WV, 105